CHAINS OFF
WINGS ON

CHAINS OFF WINGS ON

AN INVITATION FOR WOMEN TO RISE
ABOVE & BEYOND THEIR OWN LIMITATIONS

ANDREA KIMBERGER-MONAIRGY

Chains Off - Wings On
Andrea Kimberger-Monairgy

All rights reserved
First Edition, 2019
Copyright © 2019 Andrea Kimberger-Monairgy
Cover image © to Andrea Kimberger-Monairgy

The author asserts the moral right to be
identified as the author of this work.

No part of this publication may be reproduced, distributed, or transmitted in any form or by any means, including photocopying, recording, or other electronic or mechanical methods, without the prior written permission of the author, except in the case of brief quotations embodied in critical reviews and certain other non-commercial uses permitted by copyright law.

Requests for permission should be addressed to
Andrea Kimberger-Monairgy

ISBN - 978-0-6484884-7-7

Testimonials

"When I first started visiting Andrea I was in a place where I didn't really have any direction in life. I knew what I wanted and the type of person I wanted to become but did not know how to get there or where to start. I was also having issues in my personal life which I have been dealing with for a very long time as well as going through a change in my career which was very overwhelming and Andrea was able to help me to get clarity and not only helped me to set some very clear goals but also gave me the help and support I needed to achieve them . During my sessions with Andrea she was always very supportive and understanding, and I now feel that from this help and support I am able to achieve my goals and have much more clarity in my life"

Thanks
Rebecca D.

I would highly recommend the Rise Above & Beyond Coaching and Consulting service. Andrea is a great coach who encouraged me to improve myself, and flourish and live my best life.

Andrea can assist you finding out what is holding you back, guide you to overcome challenges and see them as opportunities for your growth.

She helped me to understand my own feelings and how they impact my success.

Her positive attitude, passion, great listening skills and nonjudgmental support encouraged me to find solutions to barriers to success in every dimension of my life.

Monika K.

I had a session with Andrea over the last few months. I am very happy and glad that I can connect with Andrea. I would strongly recommend Andrea to anyone because of:

- Andrea take me to the core of the problem, and help me aware of those things.
- Andrea's Knowledge about relationship and Human Behaviours is amazing. At the beginning, I have a lot of self-doubt and relationship problem, then Andrea help me to grow and become the best version of myself.
- Andrea's listening skill is phenomenal. She was really into me and I can sense her caring and loving attitude strongly within the session.

It would be terrible for anyone to not have clarity about the direction they want to take in live. It would be even more terrible when you know what you want but there are some internal conflicts within you that stop you from achieving your goals and dreams. Andrea can give you almost everything you need to take the right actions and plan your shortest way to achievement.

Many thanks and best regard,
My N.

Dedications

This book is for YOU my soul sisters, for all of you who are struggling with all that life is throwing at you:

- If you are young, you might be struggling to find your place in the world and trying to make sense of who you are and what you want for yourself.
- If you are slightly older, your problems might look like illness, challenges with your adult children or partner. Not to forget, you're still constantly on the universal quest of finding yourself and reigniting the fire in your long-forgotten dreams.

A very special thought goes out to MY SISTER Birgit, my only and younger sister who always looked up to me when we were children. As teenagers and young adults, we truly spent a lot of fun time together – we were never the fighting kind of siblings. I know for a fact that with me leaving my home country to come and spend the rest of my life in Australia, I not only left you behind, but I was not able to be there for you when you needed me the most. And hell yes, you have been through a lot, beginning with only just surviving a roll-over car crash early on which has left its marks until this very day with you experiencing the most traumatic consequences showing up as dizziness and not being able to be exposed to noise and even feeling nausea, through being in an unhappy relationship, getting divorced and then bringing up your two beautiful daughters Sabrina and Corina all by yourself (which is still a challenge until the little one has found her calling). And all of that, of course, working full time as a gym instructor and manager of a gym which now causes you aches and pain throughout your whole body. You have my full admiration my darling 'Pips', and I know that you are on the right path as a kind of 'White Witch' while mixing together potions and lotions to help others. And I hope from the bottom of my heart that by serving others your pain will lose its power over you until it subsides all together and vanishes.

Please accept this book as my kind of helping hand from across the ocean on the way to healing yourself and in increasing your healing powers for others and know that I love you and that I will always be here for you. I am only a phone call away. ♥

How could I not dedicate this book to the two most important people in my life who are the reason for my existence – MY BELOVED PARENTS – Inge and Ernst. After overcoming so many challenges throughout your entire life with dramatic losses of loved ones, financial challenges and heart aches with both your girls, you have now arrived at a point where you are asked to prove your inner strength in the most demanding way ever yet again. With Dad experiencing a stroke a few years ago and now also suffering from Parkinson's disease and Mum being Dad's fulltime caretaker, you need any support you can get.

As I am not anywhere nearby to give you the physical support that you need and also deserve, I hope that this book will stimulate some positive thoughts in the darkest and most challenging moments for the two of you, mainly Mum who would be the one reading it one day – maybe not in English but hopefully the translated German version in the near future – and serve as some sort of guidance to pull yourself back together again. I love you both so much. ♥

And then there is my darling daughter Nathalie who just celebrated her twenty-seventh birthday – how time flies – and who came to our plane being challenged in that very instance by being born with an anomaly. You have shown me from that moment onwards that you have got this! You are a survivor! You pushed through all your surgeries, learned to live without your grandparents nearby after having been and still being so close to them and adapted to a new way of life and a new language. And by doing so, you developed into this gorgeous, radiating – sometimes a bit stubborn, but I guess that is a good thing for survival – warm and helpful female who provides support for anybody under any circumstances and who is fully dedicated to the upbringing of her own adoring, sensitive and most kind and charming

DEDICATIONS

little girl who is on her way to growing into a beautiful young lady – my granddaughter Sofia. With her love for reading, I am sure that one day she will hold this book in her hands and then too can use it as guidance and support to overcome hardships – even though of course, she has always got her grandmother nice and handy to come and get advice from in person. ♥

As I am dedicating this book to females mainly, you might wonder why I am extending my enthusiasm about my work also to my son David. Well, he like everyone else had to overcome his very own difficulties coming into this world. He too was born with a similar anomaly like his sister but only needed one surgery to be healthy. But then he got challenged by having allergic reactions to immunizations which caused him to be filled up with antibiotics very early on in life. His body has been weakened in a way that he attracted Glandular Fever during High School and Ross River Fever soon after and his immune system is still now, being almost twenty one years of age, showing signs of weakness. You too, had to grow up without any family other than your Mum, Dad and sister, with your grandparents living at the other end of the world and who you know only from visiting and talking to them on the phone. With my book, I encourage you to follow your dreams and to never give up. I know that you have not found your place in this world quite yet but I am certain deep down – and you are too – that you know exactly what you want for yourself and for your future. And all I can say is, that yes, I am proud of you for the person you have become and I wish you all the very best for a prosperous, happy and fulfilled future (I am so proud of you because after two years of being committed to finding an electrical apprenticeship, you have finally made it and I wish you the best of luck for your future). ♥

Another person I want to dedicate my book to, is a very special aunty of mine. She influenced my life from when I was a teenager until now, auntie Luise. When my dad was too strict on not allowing me anything out of fear of getting into trouble, you were always there for me and had trust in me from day one that I would never disappoint you. You had your own challenges to overcome in life by bringing up your eldest son without his father and then giving birth to two more sons, one of them being challenged for the rest of his life by a brain condition occurring during birth. You never lost your bearings and have always and still are admired by the rest of the family for staying calm and centered and master of any situation. I herewith want to thank you for always being there for me when I needed you. I always knew that I could turn to you for honest advice and that helped me through a lot of my tougher decisions in life. Thank you. ♥

Finally, I dedicate this book to ALL MY COUSINS, AUNTIES and UNCLES and my countless DEAR FRIENDS here and abroad. You have all played such an important role in the process of me becoming the person who I am now. Whether we were able to spend a lot of time together, whether it was about catching up with each other once every few years, you were and still are always loyal to me and support me in whatever challenge it is I am facing or whatever endeavor it is, I am heading out to undertake. I have not mentioned any names in particular because I am afraid of missing one or the other because I am in the enormous lucky position to call so many of you as my dear friends. And if you are one of them, you know that I am speaking to you and it fills me with the most amount of gratitude imaginable (I almost feel overflowing) to call you MY DEAREST FRIENDS. ♥

Know that you all are very special and appreciated and that life is here to be lived in full with all its ups and downs. It is about growing in the moments of hardship and enjoying the beautiful times following it even more.

And it is about seeing the light at the end of the tunnel at all times, even in the darkest moments of your existence. You can draw the needed energy from within yourself because you are a holistic being beaming with warm and bright sparks in your inner core and you are enough and you are exactly where you are supposed to be.

Always know that there is somebody caring for you and providing help and support along the way.

Please feel free to reach out to me at any moment in time and where ever you might be in the world if you have trouble tapping into your source. It is my destiny and my purpose to provide you with support, the necessary pep talk, and the guidance you are seeking for, and I know that together we will reach your full potential and you will be able to find your life's purpose and in the very end YOU WILL BE LIVING YOUR LIFE'S PURPOSE.

♥I LOVE YOU ALL AND SEND YOU MY ADMIRATION FOR STEPPING UP♥

Foreword By Joe Pane

There comes a time in most of our lives where we become lost. Lost in life, or lost in a relationship or lost in our career or lost emotionally or lost spiritually. At these times of great vulnerability we can either go deeper into the lost state or we can begin making different decisions and dig deeper into connecting with the one quality which will help us regain our power, and regain our clarity of what matters.

That one quality is courage. The ability to tap into our own truth. Tap into what truly matters to us, to become brutally honest with ourselves and act on that truth and that honesty.

Andrea is the hallmark of that truth, honesty and courage it takes to look within. It takes incredible courage, and honesty to break the bonds of suppression, and incredible limitation we can experience when in a relationship riddled in control and manipulation. Andrea's courage to break free of these limits, ignited her own sense of identity.

Andrea's powerful message given with great clarity helps us learn how to navigate and work through the inevitable challenges life brings. It has been said that the challenges in our lives either become the reason why we can't achieve something or those very same challenges are the very reason why we will and must achieve that very thing.

You hold in your hands a book which is a beautiful example of where the obstacle becomes the way. Andrea takes us on a wonderful journey firstly by bringing into our awareness that we are not alone in the challenges we face. Andrea then introduces us into how we approach our problems in simple clear instruction.

Ultimately change can only happen when we take action. Andrea illustrates an array of examples of inspirational action which moves us toward becoming the person we were always meant to be.

These actions eventually lead us to a sense of abundance. An abundance rich in relationship, rich in spirit and rich in experience.

'Chains Off Wings On', takes us on the one journey that matters the most. A journey into our hearts. It is in our hearts where we can re connect with our awareness, approach to life, inspired action and ultimately an abundance of fulfilment and meaning.

Joe Pane
Expert in human behaviour and author of Courage To Be You.

CHAINS OFF
WINGS ON

Free yourself from any chains

And take the reins.

Let life carry you on its wings

To do all the magical things,

It has to offer in your wildest dreams.

That means:

If fear sets in,

Don't you dare give in.

Stay strong and have faith in yourself,

That will contribute to your biggest wealth:

Your Happiness

Andrea Kimberger-Monairgy

Contents

Preamble
How to Read this Book xix

Introduction
The Enlightened Women Genesis xxi

Chapter One
Learn your Lesson 1

Chapter Two
Early Setbacks to Magic 28

Chapter Three
Take Ownership of your Life 46

Chapter Four
Let the Wings do their Job 61

Chapter Five
The Meaning of Love – for Young and Old 73

Chapter Six
Stay True to Yourself Always 91

Chapter Seven
Pulling on One String 110

Chapter Eight
Love is Not Enough 125

Chapter Nine
We don't own them, We are Only here to Guide them 140

Chapter Ten
Enjoy the Ride 157

Chapter Eleven
Forgiveness – your Most Precious Jewel 180

Gratitude 186
Acknowledgements 187
Summary 191
About the Author 195
About Rise Above & Beyond Coaching & Consulting 196

Preamble
How to Read this Book

"Change your life today.
Don't gamble on the future,
act now without delay."

❦ By Simone de Beauvoir ❦

Throughout the book, you will find that every chapter consists of four different parts, representing the four elements of a deck of cards. The reason I chose the symbols of a deck of cards is, because they complement each other just in the way the four formats of each chapter complement each other and will give you an insight on what the chapter is about, which tools I am going to introduce in it, how you can make every chapter your own and finally, a way of how to learn from it and stepping out of your comfort zone to moving on to the next step closer to your fulfillment. I call these four steps ...

- ♥ AWARENESS ♥
- ♣ APPROACH ♣
- ♠ ACTIONS ♠
- ♦ ABUNDANCE ♦

Let me briefly explain to you the meaning of the four individual components in each chapter:

1. In Awareness, I have shared a part of my story which is relevant to the Coaching Model introduced in the specific chapter. By sharing my story with you, I want to let you know that you are not alone,

that we all have to overcome our challenges and make the best from our experiences to learn our lessons from it and move on.

2. In Approach, I have given a quick overview of the Coaching Model that I introduce in the current chapter, so that you have an idea of where I am going with it. By explaining the nature of the Coaching Model, I elicit the benefits and the positive impact it can have in your life if you decide to put the model into practice for your own circumstances.

3. In Actions, I have listed examples on how to make use of the model in real life. I have, therefore, shared real life instances on where the model has been applied successfully and on where the person has failed by not stepping forward.

4. The Abundance Part is purely for you to use for your own growth, to provide significance and gain ultimate achievement of your life's goals. In each Abundance section, I have tried to enable you to come along and join me in some hands-on exercises where you get the chance to grow into the person you want to be.

I trust that by separating and dividing every chapter into little chunks with different intention, you will be able to digest all the information to an extent where you can use it for your own welfare and growth. As every chapter has its important message, you don't need to read the book from A to Z but can choose which chapter might be of utmost importance to you.

I know you got this.

Introduction
The Enlightened Women Genesis

"Our beliefs become our thoughts.
Our thoughts become our words.
Our words become our habits.
Our habits become our values.
Our values become our destiny."

By Gandhi

♥ AWARENESS ♥

This is for YOU! And I call you an enlightened woman. Because I know you already have all the answers within you. You might then ask me, what is the need of this book at all?

I'm writing this book, just in case you forget to look inward. You might have been getting caught up in your life the way it is unfolding and very often, unfortunately, ignore who you really are. You neglect the very things that you value the most, that are most important to you. You concentrate on the daily chores, trying to get through one day after the other, whether it is going to work, doing housework or driving your children around and running the household at the same time. And then you wonder why you feel exhausted, frustrated, overworked, worn out and start questioning the purpose of your very existence.

Yes, of course if you are a mother, you devote yourself to the upbringing of your children. That is not it though, today's society asks so much more from you.

CHAINS OFF - WINGS ON

You are supposed to be the perfect mother, the beautiful and exciting wife and intimate partner, the smart and switched on business woman or loyal and responsible employee and not to forget the cleaner, the gardener, the chef who prepares scrumptious meals every single night.

Wow, just counting out all the expectations that linger upon you makes the reader feel heavy and exhausted, yet living through these tiring chores and trying to keep the energy level at a sane standard is a totally different story.

So this book is a little hint for you, just in case you forget to value yourself, or to put yourself first and keep looking after the world before you even meet your basic needs.

The Enlightened Female Genesis for me is a journey of women, for some of us and as it was for me, a voyage from a very dark place where we struggle to exist and where we have lost ourselves to all the external necessities, expectations and beliefs that other people have from us. We might have arrived at a place where we, the person we truly are and who we are supposed to be, does not exist anymore. We have been shaped into an illusion that others have on us but which, in reality, has nothing to do with the real us.

So, I am asking you to come along on a reflecting ride to where the light is and where, in the end, you can enjoy yourself and the person who you really are. It is my profound desire to make you aware of how very important it is not to just live in the circumstances because everyone around you expects you to, but for you to realize that it is you and your happiness that count first and foremost.

As you become your true self you might enjoy being you again. I would even dare to say that you got to enjoy being you again and you will then notice that people around you will look up to you and value who you are even more because they can feel that you are aligned with your very core which makes you even more attractive. That means that they accept the new you in the very moment and for the future to come until you have inspired them all with your new powerful and caring

INTRODUCTION

identity, your new values on life, your passion and joy, and your long-term vision.

Just know that it is only you who can contribute to your own circumstances and change them if you are not happy with them. And that is the exact reason why I have written this book.

And I must say, through writing my message to you, I actually realized that I have arrived at a point in my life again where change is necessary. I cannot say that I am in a dark place again but for the last eleven years I have been stuck in the same rut.

When I first left my husband, actually one year before moving out, I started to work for the company I am still with now. It is a very physical job, not many people realize how much heavy lifting under time pressure we do on a daily basis. Well, almost twelve years later my body is screaming at me over and over to stop doing what I am doing. I have had several injuries over the last two years which are all a sign of my body slowly giving away. So I came to the conclusion to do something about it. Friends would say, "Apply for another job." But a job is a job and that is not how I see my future unfold before my eyes. I want to have purpose for the third half of my life. I realized how much I missed feeding my mind by studying over the years of being a wife and a mother. And that is why I embarked on the journey to becoming a coach. My vision is to help, serve and empower women in their endeavors of mastering life.

By getting familiar with coaching and self-help and everything that is involved, I realized that I not only have to help myself when it comes to creating another income but that there are also a lot of women out there who are over fifty like me, who are not wanted by anybody when it comes to looking for a new job. We are good enough in the job we are as long as we and our bodies function the way it is expected but when it comes to looking for a new position the flip side of the coin comes up. The corporate world and society in general prefer young, powerful women (not to say that us oldies are not powerful any longer – gosh no!!!). They very often do not even consider us anymore because to them we are done, nobody wants us anymore. They look at us as women past the use-by date.

Therefore, I am once again trying to combine all my power and all my energy in making a change for us women who have passed the use-by date to regain power and make the world realize that we are the real asset. Not only do we radiate endurance, passion, reliability and loyalty but it is us who are no longer needed to look after our families because our children are adults living their own lives. We are responsible for ourselves solely and I want the world to realize that we still matter and are the actual valuable asset to society because life has taught us to be tough and kind, reliable and enduring. I know and I am very passionate about the certainty that if we support each other we will be able to stand up to our young people focused world.

At this point, dear girlfriend, you might think, 'But I am not over fifty yet!!!! So why on earth am I reading this book?' Well, my message is for all of you out there, whether in your fifties or in your twenties. What I want to help you with, is to realize that whenever you are stuck, it is up to only YOU to make the first step to becoming unstuck. And that is what I will be supporting you with my words.

So, coming back to what I was talking about earlier on, I'm not only telling you my reader that I have been in a dark place in my relationship and I have accomplished to turn things around. I want you to be aware that difficult situations like that happen over and over in life. We are put on this planet to learn our lessons, whatever they may be. We are and always will be challenged, yes again and again, it's not a one-off event. And it doesn't mean that we can relax and stay at that level of awareness and consciousness after overcoming one obstacle. That goes against the flow of life. We need to surrender to the flow of life and lean into the waves that try to sweep us under. Imagine you are in a rip and try to swim against it. What happens next? Yes, damn right – you will drown. And that is exactly what I mean with the flow of life, just let it happen. Go along with the change and enjoy the new experiences, the new learnings that you gain from it, the new relationships being swept along with it and all the other inspiring, adventurous and exciting moments. Accepting change and going along with it means that we are growing from the person we are into the person we are meant to be.

Therefore, I am asking you, dear girlfriend out there to go through these learning stages that I have revealed in my book, based on my relationship mainly. Make the book work for you as a guide and become conscious of situations in your life that are, maybe, not serving you in a helpful and empowering way. Notice how you feel about certain circumstances and start questioning yourself what it is you really want and who it is you are really supposed to be.

And realize that we never ever stop learning throughout our whole existence and it is the learning that keeps us alive and agile not only physically but also mentally. If we were to stop learning, it would mean we die. Because death puts a stop to everything.

I have written this book in regards to relationships and with this, I don't only mean the ones with your intimate partners, but first and foremost the relationship that you have with yourself. The way you treat yourself and how you see yourself determines the way in which you interact with your environment, whether it be your private surrounding, your work relations or your intimate partnerships.

Be reminded: The ultimate enhancer in our lives must be the quality of our relationships – the relationship we have with others, but equally important, the relationship we have with ourselves first. As you commit to accepting yourself as the person you truly are, you will then experience love in ways you never even thought existed because love is the one thing that really matters in life. In the beginning, presenting your true self to the world might feel slightly dangerous and vulnerable. And that's normal. Because when we show up as all of ourselves, we fear judgement, not belonging and not being loved. But it is in these moments of feeling the fear, living outside of your comfort zone, and doing what needs to be done anyway, that an ultimately fulfilled life is experienced. I am sure you agree with me on that. And it is because you share the same opinion with me on that which makes you a human being of utmost value to everybody around you. That means that you will inspire people in the most wonderful ways right now, at this point in time and in the future and they will want to come along on the ride and experience and enjoy with you the love, the happiness, the fulfillment, the empowerment, the courage to spread their wings and fly and whatever it is that inspires you wherever you go.

I have managed to get out of a very unhappy relationship and I have changed my whole life around. I experience challenges all the time and right now that there is another one waiting for me and I'm determined to approach that test and master it again with total commitment to myself and as a result, I will come out even stronger than I am now!

The way this book works for you is, that it is not a textbook that you read from page one through to the last page. That does not mean you cannot do that either. It is up to you on how you decide to go about it. But the way the book is structured is that you can actually open it at any page. You will find help at any stage because I'm a strong believer in faith and I know that if we are putting the right thoughts out into the universe and the right intent on what matters to us, the universe will guide us on the right path to where we have to be right now to find the appropriate answer to our problem.

And that's exactly how this book is supposed to be. It's meant to assist you at any stage in your life with any problem you are encountering at this point.

Before opening the book to any particular chapter, I want you to concentrate on the issue you are struggling with and then put the thought out there.

As you unfold the pages, you will then find the answer you are seeking to the situation you are in and you will find a step by step guide on how to get through it.

I consider myself as your sister and you know a sister doesn't expect you to operate like a machine. Our bosses at work sometimes expect us to operate like machines but I always say, even a computer sometimes doesn't operate like it should, so why should we?

INTRODUCTION

I am asking you to have faith and trust in this book as if it was your loving sister trying to support you. It is the helping hand, looking over your shoulder to make sure you are alright. Wherever you need help, I will be there along the way, guiding you, giving you hope, strength and reinforcement.

And I know you can do this. I have done it, you can do it. You just have to be committed. You must not give up. That's the one thing I cannot reinforce enough. You must never give up because you think it is too hard. The moment you even consider doing just that, you are giving in to your fear of the unknown and therefore, hold yourself back from becoming the ultimate, the best version of you.

So, the one thing I ask from you in return for helping and guiding you, is to just keep going. Make a promise, a commitment to yourself to keep going, no matter how tough the going will be.

Push the obstacles aside or walk right through them and intently push them out of your way one after the other. You will see the light at the end of the tunnel eventually, just keep pushing through. There is no way around it. You just have to keep plugging away.

To help you get started, please make the following 12 steps your own and see them as an empowerment to keep going when your ego tries to make you quit, because your EGO the way it is now, has not met and does not know how inspiring, wonderful and empowering your new future EGO will be:

And following are those 12 steps.

	THE NAÏVE VERSION OF US	THE EVOLVED VERSION OF US
1.	We gave ourselves up to serve our husbands and children.	Now we know, we serve ourselves only.
2.	We believed that by doing what we were asked to do by our partners, we would have a harmonious fulfilled live, instead we earned mistrust, jealousy and disrespect.	Now we know that equal respect is needed and we share chores. We know the importance of trust and respect for each other.

THE NAÏVE VERSION OF US	THE EVOLVED VERSION OF US
3. We realized that we did not exist anymore and that it was mandatory to find our true selves again to be able to regain respect and assist our children in growing up in to healthy adults.	Now we know and believe in our core selves.
4. We made inventory of the person we used to be, who we had become and who we wanted to become.	Now we know that we are exactly the person we were meant to be all along and we found our purpose.
5. We admitted that we were far off the happy track that we wanted to be on.	Now we know to follow our happy track at all times.
6. We committed to making a change, to stepping out of our comfort zone no matter how hard it would be because we knew without change, we would seize to exist.	Now we know the importance of change and the thought of stepping out of our comfort zone does not fill us with anxiety anymore, on the contrary, we are welcoming change.
7. All of a sudden we could see a future for ourselves again. We shifted that plank aside that we could not look past before.	Now we know the significance of dreaming big and painting our desired future goals in vivid colours.
8. We implemented healthy steps for our body, soul and mind to be able to fly in the end.	Now we know how to fly.
9. Our bodies got nurtured by regular walks all on our own through mother nature.	Now we know how to nurture our bodies and how to look after ourselves in the best possible way.
10. For our minds we started to read positive literature.	Now we know the effectiveness of positive food for our thoughts.
11. For our soul we started to paint a picture of the future we wanted for ourselves.	Now we know how to tune into our souls and how to oblige to its longing.
12. Having had a spiritual awakening as the result of these steps, we tried to carry this message to women who are yearning for freedom and respect from others and self-respect.	Now we have arrived at our Spiritual Awakening and we are ready to share our message with the masses.

Chapter One
Learn your Lesson

"Because you are women,
People will force their thinking on you,
Their boundaries on you.
They will tell you how to dress, how to behave,
Who you can meet and where you can go.
Don't live in the shadows of people's judgement.
Make your own choices in the light of your wisdom."

♞ By Amitabh Bachchan ♞

♥ **AWARENESS** ♥

The model that I'd like to bring to your attention and for you to experience in this chapter is the **Four Stage Learning Journey**. I love how in the beginning you are unconsciously incompetent, slowly sliding across to being consciously incompetent until you reach unconscious competence and are consciously aware of your competence in the last stage of the four. It might sound a bit confusing in the beginning but just bear with me and I will throw more light on the meaning and on the process of the Four Stage Learning Journey so you will be able to use it to your advantage in solving an issue in your current situation.

I personally find it a very intriguing way of how to learn, grow and evolve and how to discover where the situations in your life are that need to be attended to and need fixing for you to grow into the person you are meant to be.

♣ **APPROACH** ♣

Let me share with you a story of my life where I needed to grow and go through these four stages:

Well it all started many years ago when I was in a partnership with someone whom I really, really loved deeply. I was so much in love that I ended up marrying him against the odds. My parents and everyone around me warned me because of our cultural differences, the fact that he had been married once before. He also had a daughter who was nine years of age at the time we met, and he was ten years older than me. I was madly in love and I must say, if he didn't treat me the way he did in the end I would even dare to say that I would still be in love with him today as I'm very old fashioned and conservative in my beliefs. To me, the person I committed to get married to, was the person I wanted to stay with for the rest of my life.

So, indeed in the beginning I was very much in love and I was unconsciously incompetent because I didn't realize that things were maybe not quite right at the time. In the very beginning before we had children, our life was really enjoyable and sweet.

Once children were part of our relationship, a lot changed. All of a sudden, I was in a partnership where I was controlled and I was verbally abused really badly for everything I did or did not do. I was constantly watched for every step that I did and for a very, very long time. I wasn't even aware that it was not okay to be treated like that as I did not know any different. To be treated in such a way day in day out takes a lot out of you and changes you in ways you could have never imagined. It drags you down and all your self-worth gets sucked out of you, you feel not worthy anymore because it doesn't matter what you do or not do and what you say or not say you get criticized and put down anyway. I felt myself drowning and still accepted the criticism and the verbal abuse. And therefore, for a very long time, I was in that unconsciously incompetent mode where I just ticked along because I thought that was what a partnership is like. (I must say that unfortunately to this day, my parents behave like cat and dog a lot too and they never managed to change their situation. At least I was able to escape the pattern that was the image of a partnership within my tribe. Of course, my parents use their generation as an excuse because "back then you were supposed to go through thin and thick no matter what".). So, I thought it to be absolutely normal to just do whatever was needed to satisfy your partner, basically to keep the partnership going. Because that's what it comes down to, isn't it? Keep it going and don't let the outside world know what's happening on the inside. The thinking of previous generations passed on to me. As a result, I was doing everything that I was asked to do without even questioning it. For many years, I believed my life to be normal and even though I was really unhappy it did not even occur to me that it could be different, that I could be happy again and live a fulfilled life, a life that felt satisfying and full of purpose. The realization came only when a very close girlfriend of mine said, "Hey, the way you are being treated is really not normal."

Oh dear, people who have never lived through a similar situation have no understanding what a huge and intense amount of hurt and sadness started to fill my entire body in that instant. Suddenly my whole life felt like a lie and my first reaction was to push the awareness back into the dark unknown where it had slumbered for all that time. I tried to deny what my girlfriend had said but the voice in my head kept creeping up on telling me that she was right. I was not happy, I knew that and there was a reason for it. So, I started to question where I went wrong and where the problem was lying and why my life was not normal.

That is the moment where I slowly slid over to the next phase in the learning journey where I became consciously incompetent. Now I was conscious of things that were not right in the partnership, but I was still at a point where I wasn't able to do anything about it.

That was a very important realization, the fact that I must change something about my circumstances because as we know we can start making changes only once we are aware of them. It's only then can we make a plan of action which means we devote all our energy to finding a way out at that moment in time to create a better future for ourselves and our children and all the important people in our lives. And by taking all the necessary steps, one day we will be able to reach a point in life where we experience happiness, fulfillment, empowerment and enjoyment and ultimately also find our life's purpose.

Therefore, when you're aware of your circumstances you can start making changes; as long as you're not aware of them, like I said, you just keep living from day to day, thinking everything is okay and you let your partner do with yourself what he thinks is right by you, in his opinion. I was controlled in pretty much everything I did.

For example, we were a group of a few moms who were dropped off the children on a Friday morning and would always meet up for coffee at either a local coffee shop or at one of our homes after the school drop off – as you do. If you are a mother you can relate to the necessity to talk to other mums about similar challenges or problems about school, health or whatever it is you share through having children at the same age. I was controlled to a point where I had to lie about going for a coffee with these girls and of course could never invite them to meet at my house because my husband would not have allowed me to do that.

For him, it was not okay for me to meet up with girlfriends for maybe half an hour after dropping the children to school, so to me that was control to the maximum.

That was only one example of my husband dominating me. It happened in every area of my life where I wanted to do something by myself without him or the children being involved. Whenever I went out with girlfriends, I had to give him the exact time when I was going to be back home. As a result, I was always watching the time thinking, oh my god, the time when I said I was going to be at home is approaching and the closer to the time it got, the more my throat started to tighten because I knew I was going to be in trouble. And really, that is exactly what happened every single time without fail.

There was nothing harmful in what I was doing, I didn't do anything wrong, I was just out with girlfriends having fun. I was always there for him and the children, constantly fulfilling the chores that I was expected to do, being the caring mother, the loving and serving wife, the busy business woman, the attentive host to our guests in the restaurant and it was never enough.

I recall one particular evening when the children were still little. It was in our early days after migrating to Australia. My daughter would have been maybe seven or eight, my son two or three years old and I had just formed a nice bond with three other moms of my daughter's class who I'm still friends with today (except for one beautiful lady who was taken from us around ten years ago by a heart attack), actually twenty odd years later. On that night out we went to the movies. My husband knew the ladies because he had met them before. After the movies we decided to go for a drink and I arrived at home at the agreed time. But what had happened was that my girlfriend who dropped me home and I stayed sitting in the car outside my house. We used the opportunity to have a one-on-one girlfriend talk. We used to and still share a special connection and for me to be able to open up to her felt so good. I was not able to talk about my fears and needs to anybody as all my family lives overseas. Back in those days there was no internet yet and a phone call to Austria cost a fortune so that only took place every once in a while and only for a sort of short call to say that everything was okay, that we were in good health, etc. My children at the time were still too little and even if they had been older I could and would not have shared my problems about their father with them anyway.

So here I was sitting in my girlfriend's car right in front of our house pouring my heart out to her and I think we stayed in the car for at least an hour before saying good night to each other and me stepping inside. Practically, I was at home at the agreed time but to my husband it wasn't like that as for him I was not at home yet.

So, he was still awake, waiting for me to come and oh my god, he verbally abused me so badly as if I was one of these special ladies enjoying herself with other men. That's how it sounded and the questioning started. I felt like having committed a heavy crime being interrogated about my offences. "What do you think you're doing and how dare you stay out that late and so on." In his eyes, staying out an hour later than agreed was not okay at all and more than enough reason to be cranky and very upset with me.

Thinking back to when I was young and free, oh dear, what was wrong about coming home a little late? – Of course, I always had to be back at home very much on time. But that was a different situation. I was still a teenager and still under my parents' duty of care. That particular time I was an adult, I was already a mother, a mother who desperately needed some time out.

Now I know the reason why my husband was so upset about me coming home late. For him it meant that he did not know where I was which meant that he was not in control of what was happening. Just think about it, how mad he would have been if I did do wrong as per him? I better don't go there and it was bad enough how he treated me without me doing wrong as per him.

That kind of treatment really shaped the way I was at the time. Luckily, I was always surrounded by girlfriends who looked out for me because all I knew at the time, was that I was very unhappy.

But being in another country not having any support from my family, totally depending on my husband financially and having the children who were still at such a young age I felt trapped. Leaving at that time was not an option because I could not see how to go about it and therefore did not consider it as an option. I also thought of it not being possible for the children's sake. As I mentioned earlier, I didn't ever want to take the father of my children away from them, because I am very conservative in my beliefs and my thinking. In my mind, husband and wife or father and mother had to be there together for the children to bring them up. That is also what was modelled to me by my parents even though their relationship was not serving both of them very well.

So, for me there was no way out, I just had to continue on and you know, over the years you just get used to being treated that way and not that you think it's normal, but you don't even look for a way out because you believe it's not the right thing to do. I wanted us both, as father and mother, both of us to be there for the children. I could not visualize us living in separate households. Looking back now I must admit that it was not a healthy thing to do either because it was not a harmonious, nurturing atmosphere in which our children were growing up. But as you know, beating yourself up over the past does not serve you as you cannot change it anymore.

At that time, I just played along. I played my role as a mother, my role as a wife and we had a business at that time in Brisbane as well where I was actively working in and I just played along keeping my happy face outward as opposed to my unhappy inside.

If I never gained that awareness of how to grow, I would still be in that same unhappy relationship. And in the meantime, maybe I would be sick, I would possibly take medication just to cope with my life because my core self was so suppressed that I think down the track, I couldn't have coped with it anymore. I would have been seriously sick if I stayed in these circumstances. And not only would it have put a negative imprint on myself, it would have also influenced the way my children were growing up in a very negative way. I mean I did stay with their father for a very long time anyway and they did live in the poisonous atmosphere for very long.

♠ ACTIONS ♠

This part is, where it is not about thinking of doing something, but where you actually have a plan of attack in place and follow it through step by step.

That is exactly what I did and with the help of my girlfriends, I managed to get away and show my children a peaceful environment where they were able to grow up in. The process of preparation took six months in which I took one step at a time in preparing myself to leave which involved moving stuff slowly out to my girlfriend's house, having a job and saving the money and looking for a house for me to rent.

My son was ten years old when I finally left and my daughter was sixteen, a very critical age for a girl. For her, I left it quite late to leave and I do see traits in her nowadays when I am thinking to myself, "Yes she had it tough growing up, there's no wonder why she is the way she is now or why she does certain things the way she does." At the same time, my son has suffered tremendously too and he was hoping all along that his parents would find a way to each other again. Unless it is a nurturing family unit where all participants complement each other, any other option is harmful to the children. There is no doubt about that and we all cope with the situation in different ways.

Another very important piece of the puzzle in our marriage that was missing was the fact that we never actually had a family holiday. That was another thing where he was controlling us. I was aware that we had to work hard and it did not bother me at all because we did run a business together. In the beginning we worked seven days a week, almost 24/7. We were not trading 24/7 but at times it felt that way as it was a restaurant. We were open for lunch and dinner and I had to actively work in the business as waitress as well as do the books and bake for the business. And because we tried to keep the cost as low as possible that meant that we tried to save money with work that we could do ourselves. For me it was washing the table cloths and doing all the running around. I was really busy at that time and there was not much time for the children. As hard as we worked all year round, also during school holidays which meant that the children spent a great deal of their time with us in the restaurant, I would have found a family holiday normal and hugely beneficial. Every single year when it came to Christmas where we were closed for the nine days, I put the thought of a holiday out to my husband. I did not want us to do that every single year but at least once it would have been a nice experience for our children. And it did not mean to spend a huge amount of money, even if it was just getting into the car driving somewhere to the beach, enjoying each other's company with a change of scenery, that was all I was asking for.

But whenever I brought the subject "holidays" up with my husband, he told me off and said that all I could think of was holidays.

As a very sad result, our son (our daughter we took on holidays twice, once when we were still living in Europe, we took her to Disneyland in Paris and the second time when we came to check out Australia for three weeks) never had the pleasure to find out what it means to be on holidays with his parents. As for our daughter, the two times she was taken along were simply reasons to investigate a business opportunity for my husband in Paris and the second time, coming to Australia was a holiday but also with the reason behind to find out whether we liked the country and whether we were able to migrate to the country in the year to come.

So, I felt it to be my motherly duty to catch up for what was missed in my marriage as soon as I separated from my husband. I started to plan a holiday for the children and myself. I ended up taking the children on a holiday to Thailand. My daughter had met her now husband, they only got married recently, in June 2018, he's half Thai half Maori. And the two of them made the suggestion to go to Thailand which would be an opportunity for me and my son to meet Beau's family at the same time. And so we did.

Nathalie and Beau, my daughter and her husband went there earlier because I didn't have so much time off from work. David and I joined them later and met up with them in Bangkok. We stayed there for three nights together in a beautiful hotel. And then my daughter went to her husband's family, to stay with them while David and I moved on to the island Koh Samui and oh my God David and I had the most amazing holiday and the best ever mother-son time. I devoted all my time to him and we would spend the whole day in the pool or go on adventurous trips by boat. We were already known in the whole resort for having fun with each other. Looking back, I feel so proud of myself because I was able to give David that feeling of a holiday with his mom. And it is a memory that will stay with him for the rest of his life. Nobody can ever take that off him.

The last few days that we were there, Nathalie actually joined us and we were able to celebrate her brother's, my son's birthday. I organized a birthday dinner for him on the beach. Our resort provided us with a dinner table in the sand, it was just magical, we even had our personal waiter. Really, it was such a unique, beautiful and special evening for the three of us and whenever we talk about that particular birthday dinner, David still gets this lovely smile on his face and you can tell that he is dwelling in beautiful memories. It still makes my heart go all fussy.

I am sharing this with you because I want you to notice that at this point in my life, I had reached the level of conscious competency 100%. I was the master of my life and I had left my difficult past behind me, I was able to step out of that controlled relationship and I consciously maneuvered myself and my children through life in a way that I chose was important and bonding for us.

It fills me with pride to know that I was able to give my children these long-lasting empowering memories, as for my husband – well I can only think on how much he has missed out by never wanting to do anything like that with his loving family. What a loss to him!

Trust me if I say that it is one of the most empowering and rewarding moments in life when you realize that you are consciously competent. You are now the one person pulling the strings to your own life. You are the one driving the bus through your life, not anybody else.

I would love my reader to grow in such a way so that they too can experience that same emotion of pride and achievement and happiness one day, where they can say,

"Wow, thanks to reading this book I am actually now able to hold on to the steering wheel of my bus and maneuver myself through life on the journey that I desire to undertake."

In the beginning my self-talk was very depressing and negative, because I was in a state where I thought I would never find a way out. I would tell myself,

"I can't do this."
"It's too hard."
"How will I make a living?"

That might sound familiar, isn't it?

I know, it is not easy when you have no or not much self-worth left. I think I can actually describe it with one word, I felt 'trapped' in the situation. I could not think of a way out. I had a board in front of my mind's eye which blocked the view to a possible better future. I was not able to look beyond that board. My vision stopped right there.

That must be where depression has its roots from because you cannot see a way out. And of course, depression weakens you because you don't think you can act for yourself anymore, you feel helpless. In coaching, we call that state 'learned helplessness'. We blame circumstances and everybody and everything else for the state we are in. And it is that helplessness that makes you find excuses and blame. It is like a vicious circle which is not easy to escape from. It is certainly easier if you get help from outside. As I didn't live in my country and did not have family around me, the help came from my girlfriends in the way of opening my eyes to the situation I was in.

Luckily, I did talk to girlfriends. Yes, so don't be afraid to ask somebody else if you think you cannot do it by yourself.

When I made the decision to change things, I didn't want anybody involved. The only person involved other than me was that one girlfriend. Some others knew about it too and helped me on the day I finally moved out but the planning was done between me and that one angel in my life. I wanted to do it mainly by myself.

For too long I was quite happy to be the victim, the powerless victim because other people showed they cared about me and they showed sympathy. And I felt self-pity and even indulged in it for the simple fact that it was so much easier to leave everything the way it was. I knew that it would be damn hard and challenging for me to aim to change my situation. I was aware that I had to start earning my living and struggle with money whereas had I stayed with my husband I would have never known what it is like having to pay for a mortgage and turning every dollar around twice before spending it. We were financially well off which of course changes when assets are being split through the course of separation or divorce.

The hardest and at the same time most powerful and life-changing act is to make the very first step, i.e. stepping out of that comfort zone of yours. And before you find the courage to do that, you must feel enough pain. Pain that is so intense that you believe that if you are not acting immediately, your life might be over and you might die. Let me tell you that only when the pain is intolerable and unbearable, you will find the tiny weeny spark of courage to set that wheel of change in motion. As soon as you have managed to do that, it is just a matter of putting enough muscles in to get the cart rolling and you will be happy to chip away bit by bit to make that miraculous life-enhancing shift.

And don't forget, I cannot stress it enough, if you have help from somebody else it is a lot easier than doing it all on your own because it really takes a lot of commitment, courage, growth, strength, back bone, and a lot of work to make change happen. And I am not even saying to change but to slowly make the shift happen step by step.

For many people, taking responsibility seems a too big step and they fail right from the beginning. To succeed you have to have a big enough why, feel the extreme pain that you want to escape from and you must be able to tap into the pleasure, the pleasure that shines like a bright white light at the end of the dark tunnel through which you will place one tiny step after the other one by one. Staying the victim means pain, pain that you cannot and do not want to feel any longer. You are done with that and you can do that because you want it badly enough.

Another ground-breaking and important commodity is, you have to make the commitment to yourself that you are willing to do whatever it takes, to get you out of your debilitating unsatisfying and destroying circumstances. And you also have to be aware that once you make the first step, you have to follow through with all the other instances that are going to follow because there's no more turning point, you cannot turn around anymore. Yes, there is no room for you in the past where you have been living, not anymore. By taking the first action step you initiate the new you who cannot go back to living the life that the old you had accepted to live. By taking that first step, you have already outgrown yourself. So, notice that once you take that initial step, you have to go all the way until the end.

There's no turning around. And yes, I get that initially it is very daunting and traumatizing to even think about the possibility of changing our current situation. It was not an easy task for me either, especially in a financial way because we used to run a family business together with me not earning an income at all. We had a pool of money which was ours to use and share. We had a very comfortable life, no mortgage, we owned our house outright, the cars, everything, even the business. We had no debts and therefore a very comfortable living.

It was very clear to me that from the moment I was walking out that door, I had to actually make a living for myself and for the children, and that I would not be living in a nice house on acreage, with swimming pool and air condition. I would have to live in a small place that I will hardly be able to afford. It was an even more difficult and heartbreaking change in scenery for my children, there was no more having fun in the swimming pool with their friends. And what I mean by that is also, they could not impress their peers anymore by the way they were living. They might have even been embarrassed inviting their friends to our new tiny home without air condition, not even ceiling fans and very limited backyard.

For me it was heaven on earth, the peace and the freedom I experienced was priceless.

Like mentioned in the beginning, I was unconsciously incompetent for a very long period of time. I think when you are in that phase, it really needs an outside person to make you aware of what you are missing.

I don't think anybody will gain that awareness by themselves because to us it seems normal. Not very often do we question our circumstances unless it is pointed out by an outside person or we notice our life to be different in comparison with other family's lives. But then again, who says what's right or what's wrong?

As our awareness is at the level of our unconscious mind, we obviously do not know that there is something wrong. So for me really, it took my girlfriend who said, "You know, it's not normal the way you're living." And then we might even question statements made by other people because we do not want to wake up. We choose to continue living in our little bubble because it is a safe haven that we had known for so many years and that kept us safe for all that time. And then suddenly there is somebody who dares to say that my life was not normal. "Wait a moment, what does she mean? I have no idea that I was being controlled! Yes, I was not happy but that does not mean that my husband has power over me. What is she talking about?" That's the kind of self-talk that took place in my head. It was even normal to me to be verbally abused. Over the years that treatment became second nature. It was part of the partnership we had. So, what is there not to be normal?

At that point, I still saw my husband as the loving husband and father of my children. Would you believe it? But yes, of course I was unconsciously unaware of being mistreated even though he verbally abused me in the restaurant in front of customers. It was so obvious that he was doing that and I still thought nothing wrong of it.

I mean, how far down the track have I been already in losing my self-worth, my ability to distinguish between right and wrong, the belief in myself and what person had I become?

I cannot reinforce the necessity of the input from an outsider enough because only somebody else has clear insight of the situation. Only they can compare a healthy situation with the unfavorable environment you might be in and can carefully share that perception with you. It might only be a little thing that triggers something in you or maybe you see something in other families or you might watch maybe a movie on TV that causes you to reflect on your situation making you think, "Oh, hang on a moment, maybe there is not everything okay in the way I'm living or the way things happen to me." As all of that happens on an unconscious level, it's quite tricky to bring it to our conscious level.

In my opinion, it really takes somebody else to make us aware of it. And once that special person carefully approaches you about your situation, it takes a fair amount of time for that thought to sink into your unconscious mind. You'd rather pretend you are sleeping, not wanting to wake up as a desperate plead to disguise the truth. There is actually a nice quote that comes to the mind, "You cannot awaken somebody who pretends to be asleep."

You fall into panic mode and need to deal with that emotion first and then it takes all the courage that you can gather to get used to a slight possibility of change, very carefully and slowly.

The moment you allow yourself to realize that there might be truth in what the other person says about your situation and you agree that something is wrong, you become unconsciously competent. But you don't know yet how to go about the new view on your circumstances. You continue to struggle to get used to the possibility of not living the perfect life, of actually living a lie so far.

And it starts to get very uncomfortable. This is where we need to gain awareness that eventually we have to take that step out from our comfort zone into the unknown, into where it's going to be uneasy, difficult and daunting.

Unconscious Competence is exactly that phase, yes, because you do know something is wrong but you don't want to wake up yet, you are not ready to open your eyes to the world around you. You still hold back and this happens out of fear of moving into an unfamiliar territory. It is also right there where the confusion sets in, because all of a sudden somebody tells you that there is an error in the way you are living and breathing. Ouch, how come something is not right? You start to get confused. And at that stage you might even think it's too hard, "I'm going to quit. I'm going back again to my old and familiar ways." At that point in time you are still able to make that step back because you haven't publicly shown that you are about to change, that you are willing to turn what was valid so far upside down. Just be mindful of taking that step backwards because most likely that could mean that you will never, ever try to move out of your unconscious incompetence or conscious incompetence. I think taking a step back takes all the guts out of you, and you will settle for what you have at that moment, for the rest of your life.

Dear reader, be warned that this is a step by step process and each and every step has its significance and value, so skipping one of the milestones is not getting you where you want to end up with. The more you can break the huge junk of your end goal up into small digestible bite sizes, the more likely you are going to succeed in your endeavor. Take your time with waking up to the painful reality but don't miss the instant of courage as a spark in the ignition to get you going. Use it while it is there as it might disappear too quickly without you taking advantage of its existence and there might not be another spark for a very long time. I dare say that there might not be one for the rest of your life because with every failing attempt to improve your situation, you make it ten times harder for yourself to finally stay strong and pull through.

There is absolutely nothing wrong in moving forward slowly because wanting to land at the finish line too quickly might scare you off. There might be a chance of you not coping with the new situation and as a result, you might act like a snail and crawl back into your house of comfort and familiarity for never to come out of it again.

That means giving your power away which ultimately comes down to giving your life away, ceasing to exist and ending up being of bad health and a victim to your circumstances.

That does not sound very inviting, does it? Therefore, it is a no brainer to summon your will power and move on to the next stage which is being consciously competent.

In that third phase, where we are consciously competent, we get familiar with the idea or the thoughts that we must change something about the present situation and we start to sort of construct a plan and put things together. We know at this stage there is only one way we can head to and this is the way to move forward. There is no turning back at this stage anymore and at that point in time, it's very important to have the end in mind.

The question we need to ask ourselves is, "What is the outcome that I want from the change that I'm going to make and why do I want this?"

Only then will you be able to continue when difficulties arise and when you find yourself in a downward spiraling phase. You will find yourself in such a situation over and over again because you are already in a very negative state of mind which takes a tremendous effort to escape from.

Let me tell you that you will always find yourself jumping out of the present situation for a moment and then falling back again. Each time that happens you must pull yourself together again to keep going until you are happy with how the way things unfold. To help overcome that behavior where you binky like a rabbit twisting yourself repeatedly into opposite directions, you not only need to have the end in mind, but really be focused on the outcome that you strive for. You can reinforce the intensity of your visual outcome by the way to experience what it will feel like once you have arrived at your desired destination.

In my case, the outcome was to separate from my husband and step out of the relationship. I had to be tremendously careful on how to go about my plan because he was not to know what I was planning. Had he found out what I was up to, he would have tried anything in his power to either convince me to stay or made it impossible for me to leave all together. It all had to happen in secret. Out of fear that he could find out I didn't share my plans with anybody at all except for my girlfriend who was the one making me aware that the situation I was living in wasn't normal.

She was the only person aware about it all and she really helped me a lot. She was my guardian angel in disguise and I am so thankful for that support. I was even able to store some of my personal belongings in her house six months before moving out from our family home. During that time, I lived with my husband as if nothing had happened or nothing was going on. It was also then that I got the job with a supermarket where I'm still working. I chose to work for them because I knew the company from Europe and knew that the employment would provide me with a stable and secure income that I was looking for to finance my future and my children's future.

So, while I was still with my husband, and while we were still owning and running the restaurant, I started to work on a very minimal contract for that company. I explained to my husband that because our business meant mainly night time work for us, it would make total sense to do something during the day when the children were actually at school. That is how I justified me starting to work for someone else. As for myself, I knew I needed that money to save up a certain amount to pay the rent of the house that I was going to rent in advance. I did not want to just live in any home because I knew it would be for quite a long time. It was not just for a month or two, it could be for years and the children and I needed to be happy and comfortable in that house.

I looked at many places and having limited budget for the weekly rent, of course, left me with minimal choice. So, most of the houses in my pay bracket where dark, rundown holes where I could not see myself and the children live until I found the house that gave me a really good vibe.

Even though it was a draining process during which I had my doubts, I kept going in that unconsciously-competent phase because I knew exactly why I was doing it and what I was doing it for. It was very hard at times and in even the work that I was doing. I remember one evening when I came home at 10 o'clock at night, I had a long day behind me. I worked the lunch shift in the restaurant from 11 am until 1.30, got quickly changed and headed off to my supermarket job where I worked until later in the evening. (Even though it was supposed to be a day job primarily, I had to accept late shifts every now and then. That was a pre-requisite to even getting the job in first place).

As I was in bed crying from exhaustion, I remember even my husband came to the bed really nice and told me that there was no need for me to do this and run myself into the ground. While he could not understand why I put myself under so much pressure, I knew the exact reason for what needed to be done. I had to do exactly that for myself and my children. I had to bite the bullet and just keep going.

That example is the perfect explanation to how important it is to keep the end in mind and being focused in that phase. The unconscious competence is actually a good place to be in because we might be more competent than we know.

In these circumstances, you still feel very vulnerable and in fact, you are still very fragile. You have not gained the trust and confirmation in your competence yet at all. You have not left that very dark place yet, you are still working on how to escape. It is your longing, the taste of success in the end that keeps you moving forward.

I managed it somehow with enough will power and then slowly, I moved into the next phase, the consciously-competent phase where I knew that my strategy would work out. I could see the light at the end of the tunnel and I just had to be consistent in what I was doing. It was in that instance where my husband came to my bed telling me that I did not have to put myself through this, that I decided to keep going even more so.

Nobody knew at that stage about what was going on. I hadn't shared it with the children, with nobody else, I just kept on going and what seemed very hard in the beginning, seemed sort of getting easier because it got second nature.

It became a new routine for me to work two jobs, the restaurant to keep the peace on the home front and to work in my job at the supermarket. The reason why I was doing it became more apparent as I could see the money building up slowly in my personal bank account. I was sort of on autopilot and just did what I had to do. At this stage, many people would ask me how I could cope with working two jobs; also my girlfriend who knew what was going on. For me, it was crystal clear as water how I was managing what I was doing. I was so focused on the outcome and I could see that I was well on my way to the finish line.

I am sharing this with you by using a story of my life but I want you to understand that you can apply this model in a lot of circumstances.

In fact, every time you learn something new, you go through these stages. I mean even children go through that stage. For example, when they learn how to ride a bike. In the beginning, they're unconsciously incompetent. They have no idea what they're about to do and what they should be doing. And then slowly, they might see from other children how they manage to stay in the saddle and they become conscious of what it is they need to do. But they're still incompetent, so they are in that second phase, consciously incompetent and then they apply, and apply what they see from others and they keep practicing until all of a sudden, without even knowing, they can do a few paddles without falling over.

They are unconscious competent now and with even more practice and a driving force, they all of a sudden become consciously competent and they master the four stages of that learning journey.

That is just a very simple example for the successful use of this model but everybody can really apply it to every stage in their life whether it is the beginning of schooling when we first start grade one, moving on to high school which is unfamiliar territory again until when we find ourselves as adults in job situations. The Four Stage Learning Journey is applicable to every part of our lives.

In every single new phase of our lives, we are totally unconsciously incompetent of what's coming towards us. Suddenly we are thrown into the world with everybody's eyes lingering on us on how we are going to cope. Well, what are we doing now?

We just have to find our bearings and slowly move through those stages of learning until we master the new way of life again. So the process repeats itself over and over again.

This also applies to when you enter a relationship. You have to learn about your partner and your partner has to figure you out. You are both unconsciously incompetent in the beginning. The more you get to know each other, the more you step through these phases until you're consciously competent of what needs to be there between the two of you to make this relationship work.

I'm tempted to question if in a relationship, will we ever be consciously competent?

Well, it is the same with anything in life. We are on a constant learning journey, which is good. We never stop. I guess, in a relationship, you might never be consciously competent. But as long as everybody involved is always willing to try to be, then we can work it out, try out different ways that might suit both partners best and never give up. Then it really works.

This model is beautiful in reflection. Especially in talking about relationship because no matter where our relationship is, I can still take a moment to reflect and ask where am I unconsciously incompetent? And so can my partner. Awareness is the key to progress.

To make this model work for you, I want you to take a moment and reflect on how you can master going through the different steps.

What can I do about this? So maybe you should ask yourself honestly where you are at, at this given moment in time and also if you are happy with where you find yourself. If not, then there is something you have to do about the situation. You need to get accustomed with the idea of a possible change being needed.

The next question is, what does change look like?
What alternatives are there?
In what way do we want to make a change?
Is it totally up to us to make the change?
Or like in the case of a relationship, can we involve the partner?

In my case, that was not the case. I could not have involved my husband to make a change because in his opinion, nothing was ever wrong.

Of course, there are relationships where both partners are willing to give a little bit to find an approach again, which really would be the ideal solution, find an outcome together. It doesn't have to be that drastic that the only way out is to terminate a partnership in which case one of the two partners has to leave.

Whether it is you by yourself or both of you, it is indispensable that you establish a plan of how to go about it by putting steps of action into place so that the direction is laid out in front of you.

One possibility might be to go for counseling. That might be one of the steps that you might seek to make things work again in the quest of a better tomorrow.

What is it you need to turn around and work on to reach the desired more satisfying and sustainable tomorrow? It is of utmost importance to be very clear on what you want your future to look like. So spend some decent time on planning what that would be.

And who do you need to be or become as a person to fit into that perfect image of your future? Are you the ideal self that you picture in a few years from now when you are living your ideal life? Are there certain things about yourself that you need to address?

A good way to stretch yourself is to read books. For me it was reading esoteric books. They helped me gain clarity on my focus. It could be books on how to help yourself, in general every reading material that stimulates you in a positive way, in fact anything that is of assistance to pull you out of that dark hole you are burying yourself in. So maybe reading positive literature is the one thing to steer you into the right direction.

Okay, so now let's move on to the last segment of this chapter which is how to make this model your own and use it to your advantage. So what else needs to be considered to make this chapter even more complete?

It is very important to be open to receiving help from genuine people around you. In my case, I had my girlfriend who was the only one aware about my plan and she was the one I could talk to. Don't underestimate the high value of confiding in a trustworthy honest friend for the purpose of offloading your worries, your insecurities and last but not the least, your doubts.

Don't ever be afraid to ask somebody for help, if it's too overwhelming for yourself to cope with. Open yourself up to receiving support, then there will always be some help around. Assistance will and can come from anywhere, anybody, whether it's friends or family. Remember, have the courage to ask for support.

For the reader at this point, it is very important to reflect on their own relationship, where they are at. Are they in a happy relationship where they think nothing really needs to be changed? In that case, they might have received this book from somebody else and are more than welcome to use it as a guideline to the various situations in life.

They might not have been looking for the book themselves because they think everything's fine. But if they are at a point where they realize something's not quite right, then they can reflect upon their relationship and find the necessary tools and steps lined up within all of the chapters.

♦ Abundance ♦
Spread your Wings

I invite you to come along on an exercise where you will need pen and paper.

I want you to be in a quiet environment. If you like calm music, please go for it. I find when I am at home trying to concentrate on important matters, I like to keep it quiet and peaceful because we are always surrounded by so much hustle and bustle whether it be at work, when we go shopping or where ever we go. The only quiet time out, is when you go for a walk in nature but then you would not have pen and paper handy. So, please find a quiet, peaceful place in your home where you are able to go within yourself to get some answers.

Having read the last few pages, you can turn inwards and reflect on where in the model you are sitting. Is there a problem unconsciously present in your life that needs more attention to be brought into the daylight and how can you work on a plan of attack? In which step of this model do you fit?

Once you have an answer to that question, it is advisable to work out on how to reach the next level. Can you do it alone or do you find it easier to ask for somebody's help?

Are you mentally and physically ready to move on?

Be very clear of what you miss out on if you sit back and don't do anything. What do you deprive yourself (and the children) of?

What are you giving up by staying the same person in the same environment?

Feel the pain you are in right now and be assured that it will just get worse. Denying change will intensify the hurt so much that one day you would not be able to stand up to it anymore and then it will be too late.

Does it make sense to get to work to experience all the wonderful encounters and adventures that might be out there waiting to be discovered by you?

If the answer is yes, then do some serious digging about WHY you want to adjust your situation.

What does the perfect outcome for you look like?

Try to see yourself in the happy, new arena of life. See yourself what you are going to wear, what your face will look like, how you are going to wear your hair. Who you will be spending most of your time with? What is the dialogue you will be having? What can you hear at this imaginary beautiful place and most importantly: How does it feel to be there? Try very hard to see, hear and feel yourself in that ideal life that you are creating for yourself now.

Your unconscious mind does not know what is real and what is not. So create this magical reality for yourself and feel, see and hear yourself there on a regular basis, so that your unconscious mind gets accustomed to you being there. Then you are more likely to bring that fantasy into your reality.

See yourself one year from now as that newly-created YOU and see yourself very clearly in your exciting, happy environment. Go deep into how it feels to be there and hear the conversations that you will be having.

Then go further, see yourself in five years' time. Where will you be then? Repeat the whole scenario and allow yourself to feel that joy, passion, empowerment and pride. Linger there for a few moments.

Then take yourself to a place in ten years from now. Relive and feel the newly-created YOU in that calming and soothing surrounding again and notice how awesome it feels to be there.

Write down everything that is part of that new acquired you, the future you that is happy, energetic, courageous, the future you who is in love with yourself.

And read through these characteristics at least three times a day and every time you read through your ideal self and ideal day, connect to the feelings that you will encounter and let them fill your body until you can detect that warmth and energy in all your body parts, in your bones and most importantly, in your heart. Feel the butterflies that appear in your stomach and let yourself hover in this state for as long as you want to. (The more you connect with your new identity, the more you speed up the process of getting there.)

At the same time, notice at what level of awareness you find yourself in that model and work out a step by step action plan that is needed to move forward through one level after the other.

That model can be very helpful in driving you to have a better relationship than what you're in right now. And yes, if you are in an unhappy relationship, then determine if the change can come from you alone or if both of you should get involved in doing the exercises together so that you can connect at each level, which would be ideal when it comes to better or even save your life together.

Whether you are spreading your wings alone or together with your partner, there is a huge advantage in writing things down because once you have put your words onto paper, not only will the universe be aware of what's going on in your life and give it the necessary guidance and assistance but also, you make yourself and your partner accountable for the commitment that you make and agree on.

My advice is to not just write your action plan, commitment, your future self, and ideal day on a piece of paper. The impact is much more powerful if you decide on getting a special journal that is meant to take care of all your goals, dedication and assertiveness.

As you are going through this exercise, you will become aware of possible gaps between what you have at the present moment in time and what you really want and what it needs to cross the finish line in the end. You will also notice that you as a person have to change with your beliefs and values (The same is true for your partner if you decide to take him along on that flight) to be able to close that gap once and forever.

Remember, Change requires Awareness, Courage and Commitment, so start now and give yourself the gift of all three attributes to have the life you deserve.

Chapter Two
Early Setbacks to Magic

"I truly believe that everything that we do
and everyone that we meet is put in our path for a purpose.
There are no accidents; we're all teachers -
if we're willing to pay attention to the lessons we learn,
trust our positive instincts and not be afraid to take risks or
wait for some miracle to come knocking at our door."

by Marla Gibbs

♥ AWARENESS ♥

Let's talk about magic. I love magic. It is enchanting, mystic and seductive and there is no real explanation for it. So let's explore what I mean when I talk about magic.

When I was a young woman, I was very strong who always knew which way to go. Already as a child I was very driven. I had a very strong attracting aura around me. Every time people walked past my house, I started chatting to them and engaged them in conversations. They would always comment on how lovely I was. They were total strangers but I always felt compelled to have a chat with these people. I had no fear, nothing could hold me back. I was only four or five years old at the time and had total self-confidence. I can still remember the urge to chat with everyone up and loved it when they did take me for serious and gave in to me.

It is actually funny because still to this day my parents love talking about the charming little persona I used to be and how people from the whole village knew me just as that. They talked about me as a very friendly, polite, outgoing, and engaging child. Over the years, I also developed the ability to achieve what I wanted to achieve. I created this belief that no matter what it is and how hard it is, I will succeed in getting what I wanted. I can do this.

But I can tell you that the belief got tested big time when I was at high school if not to say, it got shattered. But instead of giving up, I brushed myself off and created another powerful belief which was "Everything happens for a reason" and "You can only learn from your experience". So let me share that story with you:

Throughout my high school years, I struggled big time in pretty much every subject. My parents even asked me, if I wanted to quit high school because in Austria schooling is a bit different. You can go to a lower grade school instead of high school which would not enable you to go to university.

And because I found it so hard to keep up, my parents asked me if I wanted to change schools. And I always kept saying no, even though I was struggling big time and honestly going to school was not much fun at the time.

You might ask yourself now how I could change from this confident little girl to a teenager who was finding studying so hard. Now looking back, I think the reason for that change might have been that I wasn't mature enough because I started schooling a little bit earlier than other children of my age. I had just turned six years old when I started grade one whereas most of my peers had turned six at least a few months, if not half a year, earlier. It had to do with the cut off time where you would not be admitted to school until the following school year.

Unfortunately, that immatureness turned up in all areas of my schooling. I must admit that I was very in-confident compared to other peers. And I think because of this in-confidence, I all of a sudden failed in the school environment. I also failed hugely academically in all my subjects. That feeling of inferiority controlled the whole persona of who I was and like I said, it came to a point where my parents felt sorry for me because I had it so though they offered me to change schools. But somehow I had the strength, that internal strength to keep wanting to go.

So there was still something of that magic left in me that was prepared to fight, I was not ready to give up and so I struggled on. High School in Austria is for eight years because we have only four years of primary school and eight years of high school. I was in my second last year at high school when that fatal incident happened.

It was Mathematics that I just did not get. I always thought of me having a different logic to everybody else because whatever I did seemed very clear to me but without fail led me to the wrong results. In the end I could not fake it anymore and I failed the final exam in mathematics at the end of year seven. But hang on there, I got yet another chance of repeating the exam at the end of the school holidays, in the week before I would have started year eight. You can imagine that these school holidays were not much fun. My parents hired a tutor for me and I had to study over and over again.

I was not supposed to step up to year eight at that time, I failed at my last chance again. You cannot imagine what thoughts went through my head when I was told I had to repeat year seven. It was a huge shock to the system because all I saw in that moment was "Oh my god, I'm being taken out of the classroom, my classmates who I have been with for seven years! What will they think? They will talk about me! They will point at me! They will look at me as a failure! And a failure I was, that's what I kept telling myself in that moment as well. How am I going to tell my parents? What will they say? What will their reaction be?"

So I felt like the biggest failure ever and for a certain period of time, luckily only a very short period of time, I noticed myself falling into a dark, deep, black hole.

But then I pulled myself together because somehow I could still feel that dim spark of magic feel inside me. I had to keep going, it had to go on and it was clear that I could not turn things around. So somehow

I was aware that this heart ache, no matter how big it seemed to be, would mean something very positive in my life, I couldn't explain it at the time. It must have come from the core me that still had this little spark of magic left and this spark started to grow all of a sudden.

I ignited that spark and made it a commitment to gain strength from this setback. I wanted to show everybody that I could do this. Even though I felt like I had lost the face towards my peers, my classmates, my friends outside of school, the teachers and everybody who knew me. My instinct to fight was creeping up in me to show the world around me that I was not the failure they thought I was and that I could turn this situation around and make it to my advantage.

I had a plan of attack.

Before the new school year started, I made that commitment to myself, I'm not letting anybody see how I feel. I'm going into this new classroom with all the confidence that I can find. I will present myself as a happy, strong person because I knew from the moment I walked into this new classroom I would be judged by everybody else and everyone's eyes would lie on me. I was the piece of meat thrown into the midst of a cackle of hungry hyenas. They would all run for me.

In the very first instance they saw me, I was at unease and I was aware of twenty-five pairs of eyes on me. For a moment, I startled but then the magic spark in my core started to glow and I had my head up high and greeted everybody in a very friendly way, I guess the way I used to do as a six-year-old, with the same confidence without feeling any sort of fear. That first impression made all the difference and really worked magic down the track because throughout the first year in that new classroom I was valued as a knowledgeable, helpful peer who could be asked for support and advice and who also became the mediator between teachers and the rest of the class. Even academically I made huge progress.

I remember getting an assignment back in French, I did French as my third language at the time, English was my second language. And when my teacher gave me that assignment back I was graded with a B and I thought, "Oh my goodness, how good was that?" I was thrilled over the moon and back because in all the others school years at high school, I struggled in French, maybe not quite as badly as in math, but I found it hard to get good grades as well. So for me to have a B was marvelous, it was an enormous achievement on my behalf. Well, my teacher thought differently and with a very disappointed face she handed me my work. Looking at her I feared I had failed yet again. I will never forget the words she used when she handed over my assignment, "Andrea, I thought you could have done better."

So the teacher thought I was an excellent student in French and was disappointed because I didn't achieve an A.

Like her, all the other teachers had seen me as a grade A student, a totally different person I used to be known in my first six years at High School. It was as if my identity had changed, I had become somebody else. I have become somebody, I don't want to say superior to the others, but I almost felt like it, because what they were learning I had already been taught before and therefore was familiar with the concept in each and every subject. I could use that advantage to myself and as a result, classmates would come and ask me for advice, explanations and my support. Can you believe this? Wow, all of a sudden I was the one being able to help the others. For me, it was a total new inspiring world opening up.

That's the part where magic was happening again in my life. There were a lot of changes happening around me. Not only my classmates considered me to be an authority, my teachers respected me in a way I never thought could be possible. They didn't look down on me as this little girl who was struggling in school anymore. They accepted me almost as, I cannot say as an equal, but they thought very highly of me and valued me for who I was. And of course, the more somebody thinks of you like that, the more you grow on the inside and the more you send that strength out into your environment. It is a positive spiral forward and upwards.

So yes, I think as soon as you start being stronger, just this tiny little bit, you send these vibes out and you just keep growing and you cannot be

EARLY SETBACKS TO MAGIC

stopped. Nothing can stop you. That's how I felt at the time. And really, I've never lost that ability (At times when life was tough that ability was dormant, I always had it in me). And for me, that was really very important because of course throughout life, as we can all agree upon, we experience setbacks, we live through highs and lows because life is just like that. I'm convinced that we are here on earth to grow and to learn and we can only do so by overcoming difficulties or obstacles, deal with them and push them out of our way.

They are put in front of us for us to grow and that first setback in High School taught me a very valuable lesson for the rest of my life. It taught me to never give up, to keep going, no matter how hard the going would be. And as a result of that particular lesson, I also developed a kind of faith into, not only myself but into the universe. Sometimes as a person, we feel like we are stretched to our limits and we cannot go any further. But if we have this glimpse of faith and hang on to it, then we get through whatever it is and in the end there will be help. Help will come, we just must not give up, we have to hang on to this thread of faith AND most importantly, we HAVE TO TAKE ACTION. There is no support for the ones who sit back and hope for the best. That is not how the universe works. Help is only available to those who are willing to take it in their own hands and start being active in the right direction.

Of course that was not the only setback in my life, it was just the first one that taught me the initial lesson of stepping up and turning it around to my advantage.

The next one that comes to mind was after I had finished High School with the two final years being a blast and graduating with very good grades belonging to the higher achievers of the senior graduating year.

I was left with a very good impression for the rest of my life. And soon after I had to realize that life was just about adapting to unforeseen circumstances and going with the flow of what was put in front of you.

So here I had graduated from High School, ready to take on the world. Yet the world presented itself in a different way to me than I thought it would. I absolutely wanted to study Art History, for that I would have to go and live in Austria's capital city Vienna. To get a scholarship my dad earned too much but to go and live there, which meant renting an apartment, the money was not enough and besides, my family believed in Art History being a breadless future anyway.

Clearly, I could not fulfill my dream and needed to find an alternative. As I've always loved speaking French I decided to go to France as a nanny – 'jeune fille au pair' – where I spent one and a half years which set up my future in ways I could have never pictured myself.

A few years later, I met my husband and we became parents to our wonderful daughter. She is 27 years old now and mum of an eight-year-old daughter herself. When she came into this world, I got tested yet another time on how I would handle unforeseen circumstances.

Have you ever heard parents talk about how they wish nothing but health for their unborn baby? I think we all say it without even putting too much thought into the words. Of course, you wish for your baby to be healthy. But do we actually consider that there might be a slight chance of that not being the case? Well, when I said it, it was something I 'expected' to be the case anyway and never in my wildest dreams did it come to my mind that I might give birth to a child with an anomaly.

Well, I was taught how to deal with exactly that. Nathalie had no anus and had three major surgeries in her first year. She was taken from me as soon as she was born because the doctors knew instantly that something was wrong. If you are a mother yourself, you can imagine how I felt, having had my first baby after a wonderful happy pregnancy and not being able to be with my little girl because she needed surgery immediately. First time I saw her again after she was born was with tubes everywhere, in her head and her arm, lying in intensive care where I was not even allowed to hold her. She was born with an anomaly, needing three major surgeries in her first year.

And again, I felt myself falling into a hole but of course, for the sake of my baby I had to be strong again and even more so because my husband couldn't deal with the situation. So I had to be strong for him as well. I was very blessed to have my parents' support, I could not have done it without them.

We got through all the surgeries and she grew into a three-year-old and after the final medical examination we were told the happy verdict that she was a healthy little girl. Today, only a scar on her tummy reveals what she has been through as a baby, all the drama we left behind and she's not only my daughter, she's a beautiful friend at the same time. So again, that setback turned out to be a very beautiful present for me in life.

The next whack into my face was my unhealthy relationship with the father of my children and from which I managed to escape eventually.

To summarize, I can say that with that initial set back at high school, I was taught the most valuable lesson in my life that no matter what happens, there is always a way out. And if you commit to turn your life around because you have a big enough WHY and intend to show your environment that you can do this, you can fight whatever it is and your wildest dreams will become a reality.

To help you with mastering that setback in magic, I would like you to apply the following model that I find to be very useful.

♣ APPROACH ♣

It is called BE - DO - HAVE and is a three-step model. You can imagine it to be the three points of a triangle.

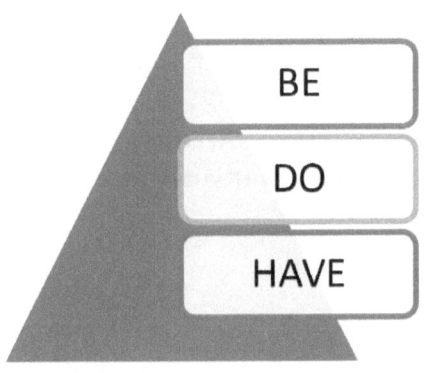

BE
- The person you are meant to be.
- The person you want to be.
- The person you picture yourself.
- The person you visualize.

DO
- The DO is the action plan that gets you to your final destination.
- Act accordingly to becoming who you want to be.
- With the DO you are setting the wheels in motion to achieve your outcome.

HAVE
- What you deserved to have from the beginning.
- Because you are worthy.
- Enjoy what you have achieved and for a new project, start the process all over again.

By learning and mastering those three points of the triangle, you can actually make that model work for you to help you either identify setbacks or even go through a setback to come out on the other side.

♠ ACTIONS ♠

I will share with you, where I was sitting with the three points of the triangle in my setbacks.

In my first setback, in the Be-point of the model I was the person that I was meant to be. I was that strong person, even though that power was almost taken off me and I could feel very weak and vulnerable. I still had that glimpse of - normally I'd say, glimpse of hope, it was not a glimpse of hope - it was rather the glimpse of strength, the glimpse of willingness to fight in me, that allowed me to overlook all the negativity around me and that strength initiated in me to believe in a positive outcome of that drama.

Whenever we know what it is we want to achieve in life and we have a clear goal in mind, we first have to BE the person we are meant to be to receive. We first need to ask ourselves, "Who do I need to be, to be able to get what I want?" What attributes do we need to look for in our personality? Can I be laid back if I want to be successful in future? In regards to a partnership, can I be miserable if I want to have a fulfilling life with somebody special by my side? Can you see what I mean? We need to identify what character traits we need for us to have what we are searching for.

Once we are clear on that, we have to believe in ourselves that we can manage it, even if it seems impossible. We must never give up the belief in ourselves that we are able to manage whatever problem there is. Some take more time to resolve, some take less time. As long as you have faith in yourself you are on the right path.

Another aspect of that Be-moment is that you need to discover the positive sides of the setback, what can be a blessing in disguise. That is very important because once you find the tiniest little bit of positivity in the setback then you've got something to work towards and you give yourself the greatest power possible. That is, the ability to move forward, not despite the setback but because of it. Thinking like that enables you to see your goal like the light at the end of the tunnel. Envisaging that target will keep you going until you have reached it.

And let me tell you that the more obstacles you overcome, the stronger you become as a person and the more you reflect on that ability to your environment which then will propel you forward. The way you are and how the people around see you as a person will have a significant impact on you because the environment forms you as well. If somebody thinks of you in a very low or negative way, it's what you perceive of yourself and vice versa. Therefore, it is more beneficial to let your environment know that you are a strong empowering person, willing to fight and prepared to make a stand.

To summarize the above in one sentence: You pretty much need to be who you need to be and do what you need to do, to have what you want to have.

As mentioned above, this model has three pillars, the BE pillar, the DO pillar and the HAVE pillar.

In the Be pillar, be the person that you're meant to be and believe in the fact that everything that happens to you happens for a reason, every obstacle that you need to overcome has its purpose. It makes you grow in the direction that you need to grow to be able to master your future.

We are here on earth to fulfill a certain purpose and if we do meet our purpose, which means overcoming all the obstacles that the universe puts in our way, then we are able to grow as a soul, as a person.

It requires faith in yourself and also in what you're doing and in what you want to achieve. I cannot stress enough how valuable and indispensable it is to believe in yourself, in the person you are, in the way you influence your environment and in the way you master your life in general.

The second pillar is the DO-pillar, the pillar where you are required to take action. By now you are familiar with the person you are required to be to receive what you want, and now it all comes down to the doing. If you find yourself having slipped into a hole, it is time to make a promise to yourself to climb out of it and get back onto your feet. You must be willing to make a commitment for the first and initial step. To make that commitment and to find the courage to initiate the first and most powerful of all paces you are required to have long term vision. Only if you know what you are doing it for, you will then have the power and the strength to be relentless in pursuing your end goal and never giving up. So having the end in mind is simply a must. It helps you overcome all your fears and doubts.

Sometimes the end that you envision seems overwhelming and you lose sight of where to start, therefore chunking it down into smaller pieces is very helpful in easing the process of getting there. Work out what it is to begin with which will help you to get the ball rolling. Once you have kicked the ball off the ground, the following necessary little leaps will reveal themselves and it will all make sense to you without falling into the very common trap of overwhelm which is the enemy of moving forward.

Once you have clarity on how to proceed, you must stick to your guns and take the steps as they are laid out in your action plan. A step by step plan doesn't help you at all if you're not committed to start at step number one, because that means you failed already. Start with number one and work your way through and to help you with the process, don't only have the strategy all planned out in your head, to put that plan on a piece of paper makes you a lot more accountable.

Even if you are not a visual learner, I find it's a lot easier once you have written things down because you will constantly be reminded of your accountability. It doesn't have to be a piece of paper by the way, you can save your ideas on the computer, as long as you can review it on a regular basis. But first of all, familiarize yourself with the process. It gets you thinking, and all of a sudden, things will come into your mind that you haven't thought about before. Once step one is evident, then the next one will unfold and so on. It is about elaborating a step by step strategy, where each accomplished milestone will get you a tiny bit closer to your desired outcome, a methodological procedure.

Think about a car that has broken down and you have to somehow try and push it into motion because once the car is moving, the more likely the engine might start. So when the car is at a complete standstill, it is very, very, hard to get it set into motion, it is almost impossible. You might not even be able to do it on your own, which means you might have to ask for help. And with the help of somebody else, all of a sudden the car starts to move one millimeter, a centimeter and the more the car gets rolling, the easier the pushing along becomes and all of a sudden, you don't need anybody's help anymore. The car is in motion and as long as you keep it in motion it will keep moving forward.

There will be a moment when the car does not need to be pushed anymore at all, because it has reached momentum. It keeps rolling and it's the same with your plan in action. You know, you just got to start at some point and commit to doing the first and initial step which we know is the hardest one to come by until you have achieved enough momentum. That is when positive and empowering events will start falling into place.

Imagine what happens if you don't start pushing the car initially, if you deny doing anything, or if you think it's too hard because you tell yourself that you can't do anything about it. By giving the power away from you and denying that first push, of course, nothing will happen and you will never get out of your comfort zone. You will never be able to crawl out of the hole you dug yourself and the change that you so much were looking forward to happening will never take place. All it ever will be is an illusion, a dream which will evaporate into the ether without ever being born into existence.

For those of you who are familiar with the Bible where it says, 'Help yourself and you will be helped,' they will know the meaning of this saying. And that's what it comes down to. You have to start helping yourself otherwise you cannot expect for some help or some miracle just miraculously falling out of the sky into your life. You have to set something in motion to be able to get that help and even if it simply means stepping up and helping yourself.

And that leads us to the next pillar, the third and last one of them all, which is the Have pillar. That's a very magical pillar, because that's the moment where we Have what we deserve, what we have earned due to our due diligence in following the process. It is the pillar where we Have, because we are worthy of having. So you must always remember that you are worth it. You deserve to have what you need. In saying that always think very highly of yourself, never put yourself down. Making yourself feel and seem less than you actually are is a very limiting and hindering belief. You better don't buy into it.

The Have is the stage, where all the work of the previous pillars pays off, it is the final consequence of the two pillars ahead of this one. Whatever good or bad job you do in the Be and Do, it will reflect in the situation that you will have in the end, whether it is the outcome that you were looking to Have or not. And if it is not the end result you had in mind because something went wrong in the being or doing, it gives you the possibility to go back and look for some flaws, something that you might have missed, or something that you haven't considered, maybe something that you haven't finished off or something that you missed altogether.

And that is why this model is yet again very useful and powerful because it gives you the step by step overview of what you have been doing. In case you're happy with your achievement then be proud of yourself and enjoy it. Keep that momentum and know that you can do what you have just mastered with every area in your life, in any circumstance.

Like I said before, whether insignificant or precious you can always go back to that model, change it slightly and adapt it in every tiny little area of your life. It is a very powerful tool.

To make it even easier for you, I would like you to look at your own life. Just scan your life through and think about whether you have experienced any life-altering setbacks. I'm sure you have, because every breathing human does recognize these setbacks that you have been through in your life. Question them and ask yourself, "Have you handled them in the right way? Have you followed a process, similar to those three pillars? Why have you failed? And if you have failed then maybe work out how differently it could have evolved, if you knew the model of the three pillars. How could that have helped you back then? Would it have been of any help at all? Most likely, I would say the answer is yes and thus you know exactly how to use it in the future.

If you have actually had the same or a similar experience that I had, where the setback turned into magic, then you can analyze what you did back then for that challenge to turn into this positive outcome.

And maybe you even remember certain situations in your life where you made magic work for yourself unconsciously. What were the defining steps that you had in place back then? Can you reuse them in your situation now? Sometimes we have to really sit back and let our life run past in front of our eyes and sort of dissect it. Look at your life and acknowledge what you have been through. What happened to me? Did I learn? Did I master setbacks that I had previously in my life?

♦ Abundance ♦

If not, then I strongly recommend you to find those three pillars and it is at this point that I'd like to invite you to come along on an exercise with me where I get you engaged in activities that will contribute to you finding the three necessary pillars - BE, DO and HAVE to transform your life from boring to roaring. So, roll up your sleeves and

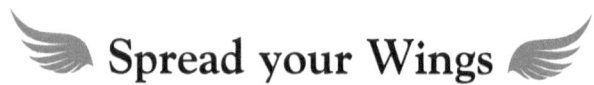

Spread your Wings

To do this exercise I would like you to find a quiet place. If you are exhausted and worn out from a difficult day at work or anything else that has been dragging you down, I would love you to find your inner calm before engaging in the workbook activities that I invite you to commit to. Whatever works best for you, whether it is a calming walk in nature, some sort of physical exercise or simply just finding a quiet spot at home and listening to calming music. Whichever will be most useful in getting the most out of this exercise.

Once you have found a refreshed state and are ready to work with me, I would love you to sit down and get some sheets of paper and a pen.

I recommend working the model from back to front.

On an A4 piece of paper draw three columns, name the first one HAVE, the second one BE and the third one DO, just like so:

EARLY SETBACKS TO MAGIC

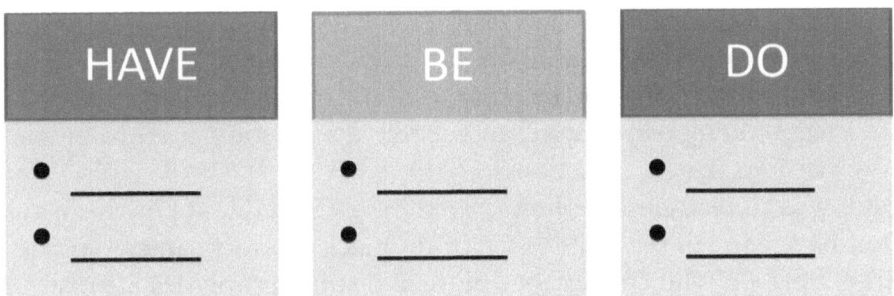

The reason why I get you to start with the **HAVE** is, to make you think of what it is you want in life or in a particular situation. What is it you want to HAVE? This pillar requires you to become aware of your desired outcome, your vision, your end goal.

Here are some questions to ask yourself and remember, we are talking of your ideal future, the ideal future of a certain situation or the ideal future for your life in general. What is it you want to **HAVE**?

What is it you always wanted to achieve?
Where can you see yourself in one year, five years, ten years?
Where will you live?
Will you be working for somebody else or will you be running your own business?
What will you be doing in your spare time?
What will you look like?
Who are the people you will be hanging out with?
What will it feel like when you are there?
Let yourself feel the excitement, the happiness, the liberation, the pride, and every other feeling you connect with yourself succeeding.

Now, that you know, start working on your second column, the **BE**:

Who do I need to be to achieve all of what I put into column number 1?
Do I have to change as a person?
In what way do I have to change?
Do I have to change certain beliefs that might have been limiting me so far?

Do I have to change my values or just the hierarchy of my values or the rules around my values (more about values in chapter 7)?

Do I need to start physical exercise to fit my image in pillar number 1?

Do I need to empower myself to become the person I need to be and how can I do that?

Do I need to read positive literature to stay focused in a positive way?

Do I have enough self-confidence or do I lack the very same?

Am I a person who can accept failure and still push on despite of it?

What are the defining attributes that are needed to represent the ideal version of the future ME?

When working on your BE-pillar I would like you to put into consideration the following universal fact:

Whatever you send out, comes about!

So, think very carefully about the person you want to be, because the way your environment perceives you, is the way it will interact with you.

And last but not the least, work on column number three, the **DO**:

By now you are aware of what your future is going to look like, and also of how the new YOU will look like. Now it is detrimental to focus on the actions that you need to implement to actually achieve your ideal outcome. Design a step by step plan of attack on how to arrive at the finish line and try to find clarity around the following questions:

Is it my environment that influences me in a negative way?

Am I surrounding myself with the right people or do I listen too much to negative friends?

What is it that I can implement immediately that brings me a tiny step closer to my goal?

(If you have a huge goal in mind, it is very useful to break your actions down into little individual steps, otherwise you will be overwhelmed and not start taking actions at all. Make your steps little bite sizes that you can digest easily.)

Now that you are familiar with how the process of the three pillars works, it is advisable to reflect on moments in your life where you have mastered the situation and where you have been able to let the magic work for you. Bring this or these moments back into your conscious mind and try to fill out the workbook exercise accordingly with facts on who this person of yours was back then when she accomplished what she wanted.

That exercise might help you get clarity on digging out character traits that are within you but have been dormant for a long time because life interfered and got you off track. It is easier to reconnect to forgotten characteristics than to create new ones. That is why I advise you to connect to the person within you who has been able to create magic in your life previously. This might be a very emotional journey that will make you wonder what happened to that beautiful you. Where has this wonderful version of YOU gone? And the emotional impact will create momentum for you to bring that back once again into your reality and assist you in staying committed to your trajectory.

It might also help in recognizing certain patterns that determined your life so far. For example, you might discover that different events or incidents have created certain moods within you or forced repeating thoughts to come up in you. By being aware of what triggers you to reoccurring behaviors, you will then be able to counteract these limiting patterns and therefore set yourself up for success immediately. Plus, knowing that you have done it before, acts as an immense confidence booster because you have proof that you have done it once before which makes repeating the process so much easier.

As you might follow the above steps, you will then notice the transformation within yourself in the most magical ways because that means you commit to creating a better future version of YOU. And that makes you an authority for your environment which means that people around you will seek your advice at this exact moment in time and they will follow you until they too will have found your magic, your transformation and your success to finding happiness, fulfillment, excitement, and love.

Repeat the magic and never give up!

Chapter Three
Take Ownership of your Life

"Bad things do happen; how I respond
to them defines my character and the quality of my life.
I can choose to sit in perpetual sadness, immobilized
by the gravity of my loss, or I can choose
to rise from the pain and treasure
the most precious gift I have - life itself."

by Walter Anderson

♥ AWARENESS ♥

To talk about how you can own your life, I'd like to go back to a time where I was still married. I was married for 23 years in total and I must say that our relationship in the beginning was a very happy and active one. For the first few years, it was just my husband and myself and we enjoyed our company and it seemed that we really complemented each other and strived for the same things in life. All that got turned upside down when we decided to have children.

My daughter arrived first and then six and a half years later I gave birth to my son. When I was pregnant with the latter, we decided to come to Australia for holidays and evaluate if we would like to migrate to Australia to bring our children up here. I was quite pleased to have sort of a change of scenery hoping that living in a country where there was only the four of us without the influence of family and friends, we could be happy because already in those early years of our marriage, I noticed that the marriage wasn't actually a very happy one anymore.

I mean, my husband and I, we knew we loved each other but there was something that didn't quite add up, it wasn't even the fact that we didn't go into the same direction, that we didn't pursue the same things. It was more something in myself I guess, looking back now, I wasn't very happy with the way he wanted me to be. I mean, I devoted myself to being a mother to my children and a wife to my husband. But I have also always been a very social person and wanted to have access to my friends even after having children. That rooted most likely in the way I have been brought up because my parents' house was always open for friends and family, for everybody to come and celebrate with us whenever there was an occasion. I enjoyed helping mum with the preparations and still love being a host nowadays.

Everything happened in big style, every New Year's Eve was celebrated in our house. Everybody would chip in with food and games that we would play. We had great music and did a lot of dancing and spent so many happy hours together. I have the fondest memories from those days and still share them with cousins, aunties and uncles when we get together. There are always funny stories to be remembered, little accidents that happened, snow ball fights and awesome fireworks that we would burst at midnight in front of the house and all the fun stuff we shared; it feels great to relive them again as a blast from the past.

And that is something that I also wanted to pass on to my children and give them to remember. But unfortunately, my husband had a very different view of our family operating. For example, for him it was not normal that I went and had coffee with moms after dropping the children off to school. And it was also not okay and very much appreciated when I was going out with girls to the movies, an evening dinner or whatever else there would be for a fun girls' night out. And I always had to inform him about the exact time that I would come home. How can you do that when you are having fun? Was I still that young girl that the parents were supervising and in charge of?

And then, if I wasn't at home at that time, he would always get very upset and we ended up in a fight. Even if I went to a morning tea at one of my children's classrooms, I would be received in anger and with silent treatment. – Goodness me! – I had only been to a school function! What was wrong with him?

And then the even more upsetting thing that was not acceptable for him was to go on holidays as a family as mentioned earlier on, which for me again was the best part of each and every year. Even though my parents did not have a lot of money, they always made sure that we had one week of summer vacation where we used to go somewhere near the ocean. When you are living in Austria, going to spend some time at the beach was a real treat, especially back in those days where travelling was not as common as nowadays. We always used to go to Italy or former Yugoslavia to be at the sea or to one of the lakes in Austria. And in winter, we would go skiing for a week which was loads of fun. And those times were always the best time for my sister and myself. And again, it was something that I couldn't give my children because my husband didn't agree with that.

Another time where I thought that I did something very special for him was when he turned 50. Because I knew he wasn't a very social person, I had to think of something else but organizing a party for his round birthday. So I had a different idea. I actually initiated for his sister, his daughter and granddaughter to come for a visit from Austria.

To me that seemed to be the ultimate birthday present that I could make for him and I expected him to be all over the moon about it. And it was probably for the first hour after they had arrived. He had tears in his eyes and was very moved to see his family. But then later on, he turned things around. And he said to me, that surely I would have organized it so that when my round birthday came, my 40th birthday because there's 10 years difference between us, I would want to go home to Austria. So I organized for his family to come out to Australia, that in return he would allow me to go to Austria to spend my 40th birthday with my family. He was so fixated about that idea that he could not enjoy the presence of his daughter, granddaughter and sister. He was blinded by his perception of me acting out of an eye for eye act which prevented him to see the pure intent of love behind my doing. How sad is that and how much did that hurt me in the end!

Despite all of this I kept living the married life thinking, well, that's just how it is.

It so happened that we were also working together, we owned and ran a restaurant that we built up from scratch and we did very well. We owned it for seven years in total and were able to establish a name for ourselves. My husband was in charge of cooking and I was in charge of the floor being front of the house. As such my duty and my role in the restaurant was of course to welcome customers and make sure that they felt comfortable, that they're well looked after. And part of that was of course, spending time at the table, have small talk with them.

And whenever I did it, my husband would stand behind the pizza oven making funny signs at me or towards me, the sort of, 'when are you finished talking?', 'when are you coming back inside?', 'you got to work and not stand around', 'you know that the business needs you', etc. But in my eyes, that's exactly what I did. I was there for customer relations. And I did really a very good job with that.

I think, you got the picture about the kind of life I was leading. I always tried from the bottom of my heart to make it all work and always thought that I did the right thing. But in the end I always got the opposite reflected back from my husband.

To me all of that was normal until one day, when my closest girlfriend said to me, "You know, the way you are treated in your marriage is really not right."

And so that's when I started to be aware that maybe there was something not quite right, maybe something was really not the way a relationship should be. So I started to question my marriage, my whole life at the time.

♣ APPROACH ♣
And that's where I'm bringing in the model that I'd like to talk about in this chapter which is the ABOVE THE LINE AND BELOW THE LINE THINKING.

So if I had stayed, if I had just accepted my life the way it was and said, "Okay, that's just how it is. There's nothing I can do about it." I would have sort of given myself up, which is clearly below the line thinking. But I changed. I chose a different path because I didn't want to settle for less.

Let me briefly elaborate on the model itself, what it means and how you can use it to work through the one or other problem.

Above the line thinking means that you actually take ownership of your life, you are accountable and responsible for what you are doing and for what you want and what you expect from life. So, it is basically taking charge and responsibility for your life and for your actions.

Whereas if you live below the line, you live in denial, you justify yourself about things, the way they're going. You make excuses and you blame others for the way things are. So basically, you play the role of being the victim.

For you to get a better understanding on how the model works, let me quickly share with you where the model actually comes from. The model actually goes back to where we all were still hunters and gatherers. It was actually designed for our survival because it was a response for us to remove ourselves from dangerous physical situations, from physical threat. Whereas back in those days, we only had to deal with physical threat, nowadays a big part of the threat we encounter every day is actually the threat of identity and ego.

♠ ACTIONS ♠

So in all these responses to threat, the brain actually releases hormones. And the unconscious mind doesn't know the difference between a physical threat and identity threat. In each and every situation, hormones are released and our unconscious mind alerts the brain. It actually hijacks our capacity to think critically and creatively. So, it's actually up to us to choose in which way we want the brain to react. Do we want to react only through the right half or right hemisphere of the brain which is the creative hemisphere? Or do we only react from the logic hemisphere, the left hemisphere?

TAKE OWNERSHIP OF YOUR LIFE

It comes down to us, how we react. If we choose to actually live in balance then we must grant the unconscious mind to draw information from both hemispheres of our brain. And that's how we can choose how to react. So simple, isn't it? We can choose, do we want to react above the line or do we want to react below the line? So in my case, I clearly reacted above the line. And I must say, now, 10 years later that I'm very proud that I did so and took ownership over my life.

After being aware of what was going on, I decided that I wasn't going to let that happen. I wasn't going to let anybody treat me the way my husband did. I needed to take ownership of my life. I needed to take responsibility of my life again. Of course, it didn't happen all at once. And I had to be clear about a plan for myself on how to go about it, on how to change the situation. So I established a plan, I didn't actually write it down, it all happened in my head. But I was very much aware of the steps that I needed to take to make that plan become my reality.

I had to come up with a step by step action plan. The most important factor for me was to have an income on my own. Because owning the business together with my husband didn't give me money to myself. We just took money out of the business. For me to have money to myself meant that I needed to get myself a job. So I applied for jobs and I got a job with the company I am still working for - a supermarket as mentioned earlier. And it was not an easy job, and still isn't an easy job. But it gave me the income that I needed all over these years.

And trust me, when you have been working for yourself for so long, it is not easy to be employed again. As an employer I could choose my timetable to accomplish certain chores – not when it came down to opening hours of course.

As an employee my worktime was regulated by a roster which was not made by me but by my boss and I had to follow the rules. To say the least – and this might sound a bit harsh – I felt downgraded as a human being. Now, being over forty years of age, I was at ground zero learning how to handle pallet jacks, wearing steel cap boots etc. And that happened to me who always made a point in dressing smart, wearing make-up and being as girly as can be.

And there was more to cope with in that regard. Separating meant a very minimalistic lifestyle for the children and myself, no more living on acreage property with swimming pool, ducted air-condition etc.

At this point you might wonder how I was dealing with such a change emotionally. All I can say is that I had a big enough reason WHY.

I knew why I was giving it up for. And so I just kept chipping away on the steps of my plan and together with my girlfriend I started looking for a house that I could rent. – Yet another very difficult moment that I will never forget, when I was at the teller of my bank to withdraw the money in cash that I needed to pay my rent for six months in advance.

I remember myself standing there demanding the money and all of a sudden I broke out into tears. I explained myself to the teller lady what I needed the money for. That kind of felt so surreal to me that I was actually there, that I had actually achieved that moment where I could gain my freedom. There was this feeling of liberation and at the same time sadness because it meant leaving the chapter of what was supposed to be a marriage lasting for a lifetime behind.

I arrived at that point as a result of thinking above the line, because I took responsibility for my life, drew up an action plan and worked through it step by step for as long as it took me.

The other side would have been below the line thinking. I could have been living in denial, telling myself that there was nothing really wrong with my life. Money wasn't an issue, we didn't have a mortgage and had a good life in that way. I could have told myself that I was just a victim of circumstances and that the way things were, was okay. There was no need for me to work for somebody else. I was my own boss. Everything was fine. All of that internal dialogue is typical below the line thinking. But in the end, the result would have been anything else but satisfying for myself because I would have been unhappy for the rest of my life. Eventually, I would have ended up being sick because of the constant turmoil that I would have had to deal within myself.

And I would have been trapped in that unhappiness for the rest of my life. And maybe I would have even ended up with having a bad relationship with my children. Because the way things were and how much my husband and I were fighting at the time, the children might've maybe turned their backs on us in one or the other way or we might have lost them by them going down the wrong road, you never know.

Looking back, I'm very happy that I chose the path of the above the line thinking.

So, now the question is for you my reader, where do you think you are sitting at the moment? How do you think you are approaching problems that are arising for you? Are you happy about your circumstances or are there areas that need improvement? If so, maybe a good idea would be to brainstorm the situation you are in right now.

Just know that before you are able to work on a problem, you need to be aware of the problem, like I needed a girlfriend to tell myself that something wasn't quite right. You need to be aware that something is wrong in a certain area of your life to be able to work on it. It might be only one area of your life or it could be more than one. Knowing this model of thinking, try and determine where you are sitting at. Are you tending to think above the line? Or are you rather sitting below the line with your way of thinking? Are you blaming somebody else for the situation you are in? Or can you say, I'm taking responsibility for the way things are?

So, if you have trouble recognizing where you are sitting, I'd like to offer some help. Is that okay?

I would like to offer some help because I know from experience that sometimes it's a bit tricky for oneself to establish where you're in your life at the moment. First of all, ask yourself the following:

Why do you want to change anything about the current situation?
What is the reason for that?
What is it that you would actually like to achieve?

CHAINS OFF - WINGS ON

You have to be very clear on what you want and also about the differentiation - whether it is YOU who wants that outcome or if you only think that you want it and in reality, you want it to fix another area of your life or somebody else's issues. You need to be absolutely certain on the goal to be able to move toward it. And believe me that it is crucial to answer these questions honestly.

Further questions to ask yourself are:
What would actually be an ideal outcome of the situation you're presently in?
What is it you need to change today to create a better tomorrow?
Is there anything that you can think of that you need to change now to have the situation you are desiring?
Why is it so important to make the change now?
Who do you need to be so that you can make the change?
Can you make the change as the person that you are right now or do you actually have to change something in yourself to be able to change your future?
In case you are struggling in answering the above questions to change your thinking from below the line to above the line, there is a way to make it a bit easier to come up with clarity about what you want. Just ask yourself the following question.
What could happen if you are not taking charge of your life right now?
Create the painful picture of what you would be missing out and then turn it around, brainstorm and paint a picture of your ideal future.
Can you see the future that you want for yourself?
What does it look like?
Who are you hanging out with?
What kind of work do you do?
And then visualize it all in the most exhilarating colors and try to tap into the feeling that comes along with experiencing such a bright and happy future and dwell in it for a moment.

Because times will be tough, you know, it's not easy to change your life around by 180 degrees. You will stumble upon a lot of hurdles.

And only if you know what you're doing it for, like me, you will see it through. I had a very big why. I knew why I was doing it and that's why I had the power and the endurance to do so.

And of course, look at your situation:
Do you actually blame somebody else for these things, the way they are?
Do you blame maybe your partner?

Or if it's a problem at work, do you blame your colleagues? Do you blame your boss?

If that's the case, you really have to take a step back and check up on yourself again.
What might you be able to do differently to be happy in the situation?
Can it all really come from you and you only?
Do you think the easiest would be to give up?

That question clearly is below the line thinking. If you think this is it, I can't deal with it, it's too hard, I'm giving up. Then know, you are setting yourself up for failure. And you will continue living the life you have been living so far. You won't be able to change anything around.

An easy way to figure out whether you are responsible and in charge of your life is to ask yourself: Is somebody else driving the bus in your life? Or are you the bus driver determining where to go?

♦ Abundance ♦
Spread your Wings

I would like to invite you to take a piece of paper to take notes. Make sure that you're sitting in a comfortable quiet space, maybe light a candle, have some soft music going, music that calms you down and then reflect on your current situation.

Do yourself a favor and make yourself comfortable in a quiet space. Light a candle and put on soft music.
Reflect on your current situation and take time to answer the following questions:

QUESTION SET # 1

- Is there an area in your life where you are the victim?

_____
_____
_____
_____

- Do you make excuses about something?

_____
_____
_____
_____

- Do you blame someone else for your situation?

- Are you denying there is a problem?

- Are you giving up?

- Are you telling yourself it is too hard?

- Does somebody else drive the bus in your life or are you driving it yourself?

If you answered yes to any of the above, decide what the problem is, where it is coming from and think of a plan to fix it.

Do you actually realize that by answering yes to any of the above questions, you are sitting below the line in terms of your thinking?

To actually change things around, I want you to answer another set of questions:

QUESTION SET # 2

What do you need to do today to make a better tomorrow?

_____
_____
_____
_____

Why is it so important to make the change now?

_____
_____
_____
_____

What does it take for you to make the necessary changes?

_____
_____
_____
_____

Who do you need to be to make the necessary changes?

_____
_____
_____
_____

How can you take responsibility for your life right now?

_____
_____
_____
_____

Do I need to involve somebody else in making the necessary change?

_____
_____
_____
_____

What happens if you do not take charge of your life right now?

_____
_____
_____
_____

And then, I want you to make yourself accountable in following through. The best way to do that is to look at your progress week by week. Check in with yourself once a week, see where you are sitting at and see if you are on track.

If you're on track, then I advise you to celebrate yourself, celebrate your achievement. It can be just by patting yourself on the shoulder, saying to yourself, 'well done', 'great job' or you can actually celebrate with your partner or children. It can be a simple meal, whatever it is, you feel is special and stimulates your senses in a celebratory way. Whenever you feel you'd like to celebrate, just do it. Because by celebrating your achievement, you reinforce that drive in you to keep going and not giving up and turning around.

And in case you see yourself off track, just keep reminding yourself of your end goal. Keep your end goal very close to yourself. Maybe draw a picture in your mind about your end goal or have some sort of picture of the situation that you want your end goal to be on a piece of paper and put it next to your mirror in the bathroom or on the fridge. Place it somewhere so that you look at it regularly and then go back to action and keep following through.

And you will find that all of a sudden, things will fall into place. It will happen as if by magic. But it's actually you doing the magic yourself. And by following your action steps through, they will seem to become easier. And because you're training the right side of your brain, the doing will have a less strenuous sensation because it's becoming habitual. It's part of your everyday life and your unconscious mind actually gets used to you choosing what is good for you.

Have fun in creating a better future for yourself and make sure you train your unconscious mind to use both sides of the brain. – Enjoy!

Chapter Four
Let the Wings do their Job

"Even though you may want to
move forward in your life,
you may have one foot on the brakes.
In order to be free,
we must learn how to let go.
Release the hurt. Release the fear.
Refuse to entertain your old pain.
The energy it takes to hang onto the past,
is holding you back from a new life.
What is it you would let go of today?"

by Mary Manin Morrissey

♥ AWARENESS ♥

I'm very excited about this chapter because it sounds just like letting go, getting somebody else do the work for us, leaning into the unknown. There are certainly moments in everyone's life where we rely on having faith, wouldn't you agree? It's maybe not quite like sitting back and not contributing at all. We do have to initiate the process and by having the correct approach and doing the necessary work, we are probably able to achieve getting exactly the results we strive for.

So, the model that I'm going to use in this chapter is the **Triad of Results**. This model has three components that should be balanced and worked on simultaneously which are Focus, Language and Physiology.

So, let me tell you my story for you to understand what I mean.

When I was in my early 20s, I have had already a few jobs because after being at the same workplace for a year or two, I sort of got restless, especially if there was no opportunity to grow further in the company. Not that I got bored of doing what was my job description but I was constantly looking for another challenge. I wanted to do something else to either better myself financially or to grow my knowledge and therefore grow as a person. I was always striving to do more, to do something exciting, to have some sort of adventure waiting for me.

So here I was working for a private company as a secretary for English and French and also replacing the Chief Secretary of the owner of the company, a man of tall build and enormous authority from the old school. Everybody held their breath when he approached. My fellow colleagues did not envy me for my chores of serving him at all, rather admired me for having the courage to deal with the big boss. Whenever I had to go into his office I just stayed myself and saw in him just another human being I was working for and who would help me get over my fears. Because let me tell you, I was just as afraid of sitting opposite this intimidating giant as everybody else, but I was prepared to face my fears and not let anybody know in the slightest that they even existed.

One could think that it was quite an exciting job for a girl my age. As for me I could not stop thinking that there is more waiting for me out there. I wanted to achieve more.

So one day, I found this job advertisement in a commercial newspaper that the Austrian Trade Commissioner in Tokyo was actually looking for a secretary. That grabbed my immediate attention and I said to myself that there might be an opportunity for an adventure and I decided to apply for the job. After all, the job was advertised in the whole country and I sure had my doubts thinking of how many other applicants would there be to compete with? Then the inevitable negative self-talk started to set in about how on earth I would get the position when there were hundreds if not thousands of other applicants. I didn't even stand a chance. But nevertheless, I sat down and worked on my application.

Of course, I had to put the best of myself and more into the application because I needed to stand out amongst all the others. To do that, I was focused and very clear about my strengths, achievements and my qualities and I was able to integrate all of that into a very convincing elaborate application.

And can you imagine? Quite to my surprise, I received an invitation to the first round of interviews which meant I had to go to Vienna, the capital of Austria. In terms of Australian distances, the travel to Vienna was minor, it was only about 200 kilometers and I relied on public transport to get there which meant I had to stay overnight as the interviews were conducted first thing in the morning. And there was no train getting me there early enough.

Luckily, some of my cousins studied in Vienna and I was able to stay at their place. Going to the interview I was, of course, nervous and at the same time very calm – if that makes any sense at all - because I thought, "Whether I get it or not doesn't really make any difference. I'm thrilled about having been invited to the first round of interviews at all because surely there was already the first process of selection happening then and there." Here I was, giving it my best. And I remember being pleased with myself about how the interview went. However, I did not anticipate of being invited to the second round of interviews because of the huge number of applicants.

In total there were three rounds of interviews. And yeah! Not long after, I got invited for the second round. So same scenario, taking the train to Vienna, staying at my cousin's for the night and going into the second round of interviews. And again, I made sure I dressed smart, kept reasonably calm and just gave my best. Boom – second round done, trying to stay as unemotional as possible about the whole situation, trying to stay 'cool' and not putting a lot into it, telling myself that if it's meant to be, then it will be.

What counted was the pure fact that I had already made it to the second round of interviews. To be part of it was already a massive achievement and I was proud of myself, simply for the fact of giving it a shot.

And Whoa! Would you believe it? I even got invited to the last interview, which was an interview with 10 applicants, the 10 closest applicants. That time the interviews were individual ones where the Austrian Trade Commissioner from Japan himself was present to personally choose his secretary.

The whole process repeated itself with me travelling on the train to our capital city, staying at my cousin's apartment, dressing smart and trying to stay as relaxed as possible. I must admit that I started to get quite nervous this time around because I was so close to the goal. I could envision having achieved it and being the chosen one that thinking of not having or not achieving it started to bother me enormously. So my self-talk changed a little bit, I was not so relaxed anymore. I, yeah, became really anxious and of course still gave my best. I tried to come across fairly cool, very focused, very polite, and very knowledgeable. And yes! Really, when I left the interview, I again had no idea what was going to happen.

I just drove home, not thinking too much of it because there was still nine others wanting the job. And as you can imagine that little voice in my head started talking to me again, saying that, from the thousands that had applied, why would he want me?

So when I actually got a phone call from the Trade Commission announcing that, "Congratulations, you have been chosen to be the secretary of the Austrian Trade Commissioner in Tokyo, and we would like you to come for training at such and such date for discussing all further necessities", for a moment there was total silence - I had to gather myself and replay in my mind what I just had listened to. The news from that phone call sounded so surreal that it took me a while to realize what it actually meant.

In the next moments, it dawned on me that I had arrived at the pinnacle of my success, not having a University degree but being chosen as the personal secretary of the person representing my country in Japan was more than I could have ever wished for!

Only a few months after being selected as the winning finalist, I was enrolled in the training process in Vienna to prepare me for my future role in Tokyo. The fact that I actually never ended up travelling to Japan and neither started my position as the secretary of the Austrian Trade Commissioner is a different story all together. What counted for me back then was the reality that I had successfully arrived at the finishing line of that journey of selection process, that I stood out amongst so many other applicants with my knowledge and my personality.

♣ APPROACH ♣

And it is at this point where I would like to explain why I chose the model - the **TRIAD OF RESULTS** to help my readers in dealing with a certain problem in their lives because I consider this particular model as a very powerful tool to attract exactly what you want for yourselves.

It consists of three components which are **FOCUS, LANGUAGE, PHYSIOLOGY.**

Have you ever heard of the saying, 'What you focus on, is what you get'? That is not just an old woman's tale, it is nothing but bare truth. If you focus on failure, that is what will happen, if you focus on having success, being successful will describe your circumstances.

Your language creates your reality which means whatever escapes your mouth will be the creator of your life. Keep using negative language and it is negativity which will come into your life, keep using positive language and you will attract all the wonderful and inspiring events into your existence.

Physiology is the way you hold yourself, it is your body language and is a very powerful component in your life. It is the way the outside world perceives you as. When you watch people passing by, you will notice the difference in their physiology, some will hold themselves upright with a certain jump in their walk. Notice the level of energy that surrounds them as opposed to people who carry their head down and slouch their whole body with an uncertainty in their stride, almost too insecure to set the next foot in front of the other. Isn't it amazing how differently they come across and what an enormous different 'language' their bodies communicate? Isn't it obvious to you – if you think about it – how you want to be perceived? Who would not choose the first appearance over the latter?

♠ ACTIONS ♠

FOCUS

'It is during our darkest moments
That we must focus on light.'

By Aristotle

The Oxford Dictionary defines **Focus** as 'the Centre of Interest or Activity'.

What you focus on, you get. The main thing when we focus on something is to realize that we should not be doing anything based on feelings, simply because feelings lie to us. For example, if you build a house in a bad or careless mood, your house will be unstable and a mess. It won't be there for you in times of storm.

The same is applicable for our lives. If we are in a sad or bad mood, we better don't make serious decisions of importance. We better take the time and wait until the clouds have disappeared and we are in a clear state of mind and in a quiet space again in which we own ourselves. If we act on feelings, all we want is to avoid uncertainty. We are afraid of not knowing what comes next. Therefore, we tend to rather focus on things we know for sure, things that are familiar to us. But all that does, is keeping us in survival mode which means that we are getting stuck in a rut. We don't actually move forward, we stay in our comfort zone. What we really need to focus on is our purpose and our intention.

And that means we have to focus on what we want to create for our lives. We have to be very clear on that. And what helps with that is, the more vision we have, the more we focus on our vision and the more extraordinary our lives will turn out. So focus is one-third of the equation to find a fulfilled and happy state of being.

The focus I had envisioned in my story was that I wanted that particular job, no matter what I did to make it become a reality.

The second part of the triangle to happiness is

LANGUAGE

'The development of language is part of the development of the personality, for words are the natural means of expressing thoughts and establishing understanding between people.'

By Maria Montessori

According to the Cambridge Dictionary, **Language** is a 'System of Communication by speaking, writing, or making signs in a way that can be understood, or any of the different Systems of Communication used in particular regions.'

Anthony Robbins actually distinguishes in his book, "Awaken the Giant Within" that there are two types of language; the **destructive language** and **empowering language**.

Keeping that in mind, you need to realize that your language actually creates **your** reality, not anybody else's. That means, what you think is real, is not necessarily something that is real for somebody else. And very important, in terms of language is **gratitude**. Not only for everything in your life you own and have at this moment in time but for every experience, good or bad from the past.

Melody Beattie said, "Gratitude makes sense of our past, brings peace for today and creates vision for tomorrow."

Doesn't that statement make total sense? I find it very helpful because clearly without learning from our mistakes in the past, without accepting our presence in a grateful way and looking into the future without vision, what can we expect? What I mean by that is, don't have only gratitude for your own life and for all that you own. I mean, express gratitude even to others, say thank you to everybody and acknowledge them and compare your situation with others who are so much worse off than you.

I cannot reinforce enough how absolutely and totally necessary it is to show gratitude and to also practice gratitude as often as you can. You are able to do that by simply saying the words 'Thank you' in your mind over and over again.

In terms of 'language', try to avoid the words 'What if'. That is very disempowering language. Ask questions and be engaged in the conversation. That shows your partner that you are actually listening attentively to what is being said. And when you are talking, make sure that you have a positive approach and are aware of your internal dialogue. What is it actually that you're telling yourself all the time? Is it that you're telling yourself 'I'm a failure', 'I can't do this', 'It's too hard', or is it actually, 'Yes! I'm going to try this because I know I can do this' – two very different approaches with just the opposite outcome if practiced over time.

And then, there are certain words that you want to be very careful in using. For example, instead of saying, 'Maybe, let me think about it', or 'I'm not so sure', 'I really should' try to say, 'I now choose to…'. That is a much more empowering phrase that allows you to play out your future in whatever way you want to without being too harsh with yourself and putting too much pressure onto your own persona.

In neuro-linguistic programming, we talk about model operators of necessity and model operators of possibility.

Model operators of necessity	Model operators of possibility
I must	I could
I have to	I can
I got to	I like to
I should	I love to
I need to	I choose to

Have a little play with the words in either column and notice the different weights that the words put onto your current state of mind. Isn't it true that the words which form the model operators of necessity weigh you down and feel like a burden on your shoulders? Very interesting to realize is also the fact that they do not only make you feel down, they have even the same impact on your partners in conversation. If you keep using these kinds of words, you have a very tiring effect on people.

Feeling the weight they put onto your very being, can you imagine what effect they will have on all your decisions, goals and plans? Wouldn't you agree that they may hold you back from experiencing the extraordinariness of your future?

And then there are the model operators of possibility. How did they make you feel when saying them out loud? Aren't they elevating, inspiring and easy to conform with? Isn't it a pleasure to execute whatever follows? These expressions may even get you unstuck from something you were not able to escape for a long time. They are very powerful if used on a regular basis.

The language I used back in the story that I shared was the language of model operators of possibility - 'I can do this'. By repeating these words in my mind I didn't put any pressure on myself and at the same time, I created a possibility for it to happen.

That brings us to the last and third component of the triad which is

PHYSIOLOGY

This means our Body Language, the way we hold ourselves.

"Although our body language governs
the way other people perceive us,
our body language also governs
how we perceive ourselves and
how those perceptions become reinforced
through our own behavior, our interactions,
and even our physiology."

By Amy Cuddy

The Collins Dictionary defines **Physiology** as 'the Scientific Study of how People's and Animals' bodies function, and of how plants function.

The only thing I'd like to say is, think about yourself going into a job interview.

First, see yourself attending that interview slouching, tired, bored, not well groomed and frowning. Needless to say, you will be perceived in a negative way by the person interviewing you. The outcome is evident, isn't it?

Now see yourself in the same situation upright, chatty, well groomed and with an open welcoming smile on your face.

The difference in appearance is self-explanatory and so is the perception of the person interviewing you because it is your aura that reinforces your appearance whichever way you choose to show up.

How do you think I was showing up to my interviews? I was certainly well groomed, I was positive, I was friendly, I always had a smile on my face despite the tension and nervousness happening on the inside of me. The way you hold yourself assists in influencing your environment in a favorable way.

Having a deeper understanding of how the three components of the Triad of Results can and will influence our lives in whichever way we choose, will hopefully make it easier for you, my dear reader, to resolve the problem that you are experiencing right now.

There is a nice saying that I've found,
"Life is like a flute.
It may have many holes and emptiness
but if you work on it carefully,
it can play magical melodies."

So, getting these three components right means that your wings will take you anywhere you want them to take you. Let them do their job and take you on a magical journey accompanied with an enchanting melody and enjoy the ride.

♦ Abundance ♦
Spread your Wings

For you to get to work, I would suggest you to find a quiet place, light a candle, have some soft music playing in the background or if you prefer, just go for a walk in nature and think about what it is you want your future to look like.

Are you ready to let go of the old person?

Then here's what you need to do, when you are at home and near something to write, you can make your notes in the book or on a separate piece of paper which you can pin onto the mirror in your bathroom, whatever you prefer.

Remember: 'What you focus on you get, so be very careful what you wish for.'
Write your focus down in **big bold letters**.
The key is, to condition your focus to be **positive**.

My Focus is:

_____
_____
_____

When it comes to **Language,** I invite you to be very mindful of the words you choose for at least a whole week.

Do you use a lot of terms of necessity? - If yes, be aware of what to say instead.

During the week, as you watch your language, write down your terms of necessity that come to your attention as you use them repeatedly, and in the column next to it, put words of possibility you can substitute them with.

Terms of Necessity	Terms of Possibility

Physiology:

Over that week, watch how you show up.
I advise to do mirror work.
Every day, three times a day, look at yourself in the mirror and:

"Smile at yourself" − "Stand upright" − "Pull your shoulders back"

"Be kind to yourself" − "Be happy and in love with what you see in the mirror"

What you see, is the ♥ **BEAUTIFUL PRECIOUS YOU** ♥

Once you have done that for one week, do it for another week, and notice the difference in the language you use and the change in your physiology.

Continue this weekly routine until
- your focus, language and physiology are in tune with each other,
- you notice a change in yourself,
- other people comment on seeing a change in you and
- ultimately your circumstances start to change.

Chapter Five
The Meaning of Love – for Young and Old

"Love myself I do. Not everything,
but I love the good as well as the bad.
I love my crazy lifestyle, and
I love my hard discipline.
I love my freedom of speech and
the way my eyes get dark when I'm tired.
I love that I have learned to trust people
with my heart, even if it will get broken.
I am proud of everything that I am and will become."

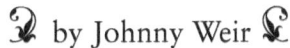
by Johnny Weir

♥ AWARENESS ♥

The story that I would like to share with you now is again one that takes us back to when I was quite young. You might wonder why I like to dwell in those days.

There is a very simple explanation to your question. To understand where I am coming from, I want you, my reader, to know that I had a very protective upbringing.

My parents have always been very understanding and I am in a favorable position to say that still to this day they are alive – at the other end of the world though - and they are very supportive and hardly ever judgmental of what I was or of what I am about to do. Of course, I did get questioned many times over the years about certain decisions made by me and they would make me aware of the fact that I might be in the wrong.

There was only one instance that I can recall where a break of a couple of months occurred between my parents and myself during which we did not communicate with each other at all. I'll get to that later. Other than that, they would only share their opinion with me when they thought that I was about to make an error. But, hey, isn't that what good parents are supposed to be doing anyway? Aren't we all trying to protect our children from making mistakes even though we know that each and every one of us has to overcome their own challenges to be able to grow?

Well, I was taught at a very young age that only the sky is the limit and that I had gifts dormant in me which my parents would have loved to see me make use of and that there were other things that I was not so good at. But my parents always left it up to me to find out what these strengths and weaknesses were. So, I grew up, exploring myself and believing in myself, believing in the fact that if I put all my intention and attention to a project or a plan, I could and definitely would achieve it and rise above as a winner.

Of course, I had to fight my battles which you have found out reading already or still will come across later in the book. But in general, life for me growing up in my parents' house was a blessing and I could not have asked for any better circumstances or any better care-takers who filled my life with so much love, appreciation, connectedness, protection and also self- discipline.

I can truly say that at that time I was in love with myself. – I am not talking about my teenage years where I hated certain parts of my body, especially my crooked nose, my too big bottom, pimples in my face and so on. Having left this period behind me, I was in the lucky position to accept myself the way our creator has made me and fully embrace life the way it happened.

I was very playful at the time, trying different things – as we all do, never anything entirely silly and unacceptable though as I was taught good and healthy values. When it came to dating men, I do admit that early on I would date more guys at once and always for a very short period of time because to me, there was no other true love than the love for myself. So, dating someone fell under playing a game more or less back in those days.

That area of playfulness ended abruptly with meeting my husband. He was the owner of a restaurant where my real estate broker took me after looking at a prospective apartment for me to move into and I was attracted to him immediately. I was still in the old mode of enjoying being admired and courted and it would have never occurred to me that he would be interested in anything more.

Over the course of six month though I fell deeply in love with him and that was also the time when I had a falling out with my parents over a period of two months because I had to break the news to them that I would no longer pursue my career goal of going to Tokyo. Instead I was going to move in with an Arabian man who was ten years older than me, still married at the time and who also had a nine-year-old daughter from that marriage.

As for myself, nothing else mattered than being with my new flame because I had madly fallen in love with him. All I wanted was to be with and around him and I was prepared to take on the world, no matter what. I was ready to overcome any obstacle there might be and I maybe even challenged myself to prove to the world and everybody who warned me of going into that relationship that I could and would make it work.

And, oh boy, there were countless challenges coming our way.

In the beginning of our first year of living together, his sixteen-year-old, spoiled, rotten nephew came to live with us for a whole year, only eight years younger than I was.

His sister with two more children who were nine and twelve at the time came to stay with us for a substantial time as well, having fled their country of origin because it was war rattled.

I was more than happy to help my partner's family knowing that they had it tough and we were able and in the lucky position to help them and I grew very fond of them very quickly and still love them to this day. What I am saying though is, that having strangers come and live with you in the very beginning of a relationship is, maybe, not the most favorable way of getting to know each other.

At this stage in my life, I started to shift into a pattern which I was to follow for a very long period of my life. I fell into the role of the 'helper'. Knowing that my partner and his family had been through a lot because of political circumstances in their home country, I changed from being a person only having to look after herself and only having to be strong just for herself into the role of "I am strong enough to be able to help these poor people", the role of the Samaritan and thus starting to make myself depend on my partner.

The beginning of my loss of independence occurred with the birth of my first born, my daughter three years later.

In Austria at the time, women having a child were able to stay at home from work on motherhood leave for an entire two years which allowed you to fully focus on your child which I found great at the time. On the other hand, I think it plays a big part in women losing their self-esteem because you don't get to interact with people other than mums with the same problems. You sort of live in a 'baby world' which certainly has its advantages and disadvantages.

I realized that I was giving myself up more and more and when my daughter was three years of age I decided to leave my husband – we got married when our daughter was one and a half years old – and lived by myself for a whole year. I got myself a full-time job and had my daughter in kindergarden in the morning and in the afternoon, my parents looked after her. Life seemed to be good except for the fact that I never wanted my child to grow up without her father. And when he promised me to change and not work so much anymore and spend more time with us, I decided to move back in with him.

We decided to have another child and soon after my son was born and when he was only eight months, we migrated to Australia.

There went my independence!

Looking at the ADULT GROWTH MODEL, which I will explain down below, I plummeted from the state of 'Realization' where I lived my life to the fullest back into the state of 'Reliance' where I made myself dependent on my husband without even being aware of what had happened to me.

♣ APPROACH ♣

The same might be true for you, my dear reader and that is why I would like to introduce to you this very helpful model which is called

The **ADULT GROWTH MODEL** where we go through different stages, depending on how developed we are in the sense of looking at the world around us.

The four stages of the model are:
RELIANCE – REBELLION – RESULTS – REALIZATION

The model is not about content, not about what we know if we have studied. It is about our level of awareness, about the level of consciousness of the world, it is about how we relate to the world and how we think the world relates to us.

It helps recognize the developmental stages of adults and each of the levels has two sides to them, a functional and a dysfunctional one which I will explain in more detail in the following pages.

RELIANCE

is the stage of children, them relying on their parents. By the age of eight or nine, we all are supposed to have grown out of this stage which is only the case under ideal circumstances of course.

As adults we can find ourselves in just the same stage, either we have not grown out of our childhood reliance yet at all or we fell back into it again.

The typical adult in that stage of the Adult Growth Model relies on pay checks therefore limiting their income. They rely on the company they are working for or on their business and even on society. They have not reached their maturity yet.

And it is not only people who are not mature yet who dwell in this part of the Adult Growth Model. Every successful person who is prepared to take on a new challenge in their life starts at this point of the model again until they move to REALIZATION after having mastered all other levels as they learn and get familiarized with whatever that new adventure throws at them.

REBELLION
is the part of the model, where adults rely on whatever they feel is letting them down, be it circumstances or people. They blame everything and everybody else for their current situation. They bitch and moan until they come to the conclusion that the only person in the whole wide world who can help them change anything, is themselves. Then they move on to the next stage which is

RESULTS
Adults who have arrived at this level of the model, are sick and tired of being stuck. They do anything and everything to move on. They are willing to make sacrifices and do whatever it takes to change their unsatisfying situation and take action to achieve full potential, and at some point, along their journey they realize that there is more, and that is when they reach the climax of their REALIZATION.

REALIZATION
They are at the pinnacle of their success and know now that this is not the end. There is so much more they can achieve, and they start looking for the next challenge in life where they then start going through the whole Adult Growth Model again.

Now, let us take a closer look at how the different stages of the Adult Growth Model work and how you can move through them and use them to your advantage on your way to either mastering a problem you encounter at the moment or just on your way to growing into a happier, more fulfilled, wonderful human being who is willing to do whatever it takes to reach the ultimate state of full acceptance of the circumstances you have created.

So, here is how I would summarize my experience of love:

YOUNG – IN LOVE WITH MY MAN
OLD – IN LOVE WITH MYSELF

And I want to assure you, whether young or old, you do not need to wait and learn the lessons the hard way. I give you all the permission you were ever waiting for, to fall in love with yourself.

But the main question remains, are you ready to do what it takes and create the following reality for yourself?

YOUNG OR OLD – ALWAYS IN LOVE WITH YOURSELF

♠ ACTIONS ♠
There are four stages.

1. RELIANCE

"It takes a village to raise a child" – but only if you are willing to rely on others and receive support that is available.

The Cambridge Dictionary describes Reliance as 'the **State of Depending on or Trusting in something or someone**'.

The BENEFITS of that state are:
- When we rely on someone, it is an indication of our trust in them or vice versa.
- When someone allows you to rely on them, it is a sign of their service or compassion for you.
- It allows us to utilise people's resources when done in the right balance.
- It allows us to focus on our expertise while others focus on theirs.

- It allows us to reach out for help in areas of life where we're not quite the experts.
- When you start a new job, you rely on your team members to bring you up to speed.
- When you get married into a family, you rely on your spouse and the family members to make you welcome and comfortable.
- And likewise, when you go through a troubled relationship, you rely on somebody to guide you through the challenges.

So clearly, reliance must be a good thing. Do you realize that people in general hesitate in asking for help? Because they think they should be able to do it by themselves. Reliance is looked down upon. And it is considered a sign of weakness. Almost as if you're not good enough if you can't do ALL the things on the planet. Take a moment to pause and reflect upon your own views/beliefs about reliance. And how is it playing a role in your life?

And at this point, I want to introduce the fact that every coin has two sides and so does reliance, just like any other human quality. Reliance has a functional and a dysfunctional side to it.

Here are some examples of how things and situations can be turned around. The potential is both ways, if not handled carefully and without awareness, unfortunately we might stay stuck to what does not serve us, the dysfunctional side of the coin.

DYSFUNCTIONAL RELIANCE	FUNCTIONAL RELIANCE
I had a girlfriend who after having had a car accident totally refused to drive for nearly a year. This meant that school drop-offs and pick-ups had become the compulsory duty of her husband.	My girlfriend should have realized that the problem clearly lied within herself and to solve her problem she could have asked her husband to help her get through her anxiety by sitting next to her for the first few times of her driving again.
A partner who does not want the other partner to go out because of dinner not getting prepared.	A partner who asks for the recipe and then cooks dinner by himself.

DYSFUNCTIONAL RELIANCE	FUNCTIONAL RELIANCE
A family who is never interacting with other families to avoid influences from the outside and only interacts with each other.	A family who loves entertaining together with others so that everybody has their fun.
One of the partners in a relationship refuses to work because it is more convenient to stay at home and enjoy life at the expense of their other half.	Both partners rely on each other's income to get ahead.

Can you recognize any similarities with yourself or your partner? If yes, are you ready to move out of this stage and on to the next one? Are you ready to evolve and grow as a person? If you have answered any of these questions with yes, you will find an exercise at the end of this chapter to move forward. - The decision is yours.

2. REBELLION

"Everything I was told should be my greatest insecurities and weaknesses,
everything that I've been labelled - short, nerdy, skinny, weak, impulsive, ugly, tomboy, poor, rebel, loud, freak, crazy - turned out to be my greatest strengths.
I didn't become successful in spite of them.
I became successful because of them."

> by AJ Lee (retired professional wrestler and American author)

According to the dictionary, **Rebellion is 'the action or process of resisting authority, control, or convention.'**

The BENEFITS of this state are:
Wow, the quote from AJ Lee says it all, how powerful can rebellion be! So, by rebelling against how she was seen, AJ Lee became a very successful wrestler. If we rebel against something, it can mean that we create a new trend. Rebellion can lead to innovation. It is the counter

thinking to an already established process. For example, if scientists did not constantly rebel against existing inventions there would be no electricity, no cars and no cures for illness, etc. It has proven to enhance the lives of entire nations throughout history. Rebellion brings about strengths never to be imagined. It propels us forward.

In a relationship, rebellion might bring about a nice draft of fresh air spicing things up. Partners rebelling against their parents can create a wonderful new structure for their family, their own way of how they want their children to grow up. They leave the old ways and create a new trend and therefore new possibilities for their children. So again, rebellion is something wonderful and very efficient to create change if it is done for the right reasons.

Now I would like to invite you again to take a moment and reflect on your own experiences with rebellion. Have you ever rebelled against something? How did that work out for you? And like everything in life, like plus and minus, there are also two opposing versions of rebellion, the one that serves us on our journey and propels us forward, and its counter-part that holds us back from achieving our ultimate goals. We speak about dysfunctional and functional rebellion.

DYSFUNCTIONAL REBELLION	FUNCTIONAL REBELLION
You are unhappy with your circumstances, instead of being proactive, you start to drink or any other addiction.	You are unhappy with your circumstances and stand up for yourself and are determined to change things around.
Your partner does not like what you serve him for dinner and you start an argument.	Your partner nags about your cooking, so you tell him to cook for himself next time.
You want to go out with friends but your partner does not want to look after the children so you are unhappy and stay at home.	In the same situation you accept the fact that your partner does not want to look after the children and you organize a babysitter.

If at this point you realize that you are stuck in dysfunctional rebellion, here is three tips on how to switch from dysfunctional to functional rebellion:

1. Be prepared to take action.
2. Think of what it is YOU want and what serves you best.
3. If you are scared of change, feel the fear and do it anyway.

3. RESULTS

"Growth is never by mere chance;
it is the result of forces working together."

by James Cash Penney

The Cambridge Dictionary defines Results as 'Something that happens or exists **because** of something else'.

The BENEFITS of this state are:
The human species is result-driven. We use results to measure our progress which means they are a driving force for us to move forward. Without striving for results we would stagnate.

In the context of relationships, results allow us to take inventory on the decisions we made. Results are the outcome of combined effort. Whether it be in a company environment or family environment, the more everybody involved helps each other, the more satisfying the results will be. To achieve results we create change. Change creates choices and effectiveness and ultimately it means a new beginning. Because after having achieved the desired results, we start looking for something new to create results again. Envisioning the desired results can be used as a catalyst for relentless effort. As human beings, we are measured by our results from a very young age until the day we die. And to make life a wonderful, fulfilling and satisfying experience we better be kind to ourselves and do not hesitate to ask for somebody else's help if things get tough.

This leads us to the two versions of results which are again dysfunctional and functional results. And to help you understand the difference, here again a few examples on how the two opposite choices of result can play a positive or negative role.

DYSFUNCTIONAL RESULTS	FUNCTIONAL RESULTS
A child being brought up by one parent is not given its full potential because one part is missing.	A child being brought up by both parents reflects yin and yang.
If you want to run the distance of a marathon all by yourself it is a lot harder to get to the finish line.	Running a marathon with many other competitors who are struggling the same way as you, makes it more likely for you to overcome the pain and endurance.
In a marriage one alone cannot be the reason for a good co-existence.	A marriage needs two people to make it work.
Children will not succeed in growing up by themselves, nor can they look after themselves at a young age.	They need their parents and a healthy environment to grow into sensitive adults.

To make it easier for you to truly achieve the desired results, here are **the following three tips:**

1. Use others trying to achieve the same results as you as a catalyst.
2. If you feel stuck, know that you require change.
3. Achieving the result is never the end, it is a new beginning.

This brings us to our last developmental stage, the ...

4. REALIZATION

"What you get by achieving your goals
is not as important as
what you become by achieving your goals."

by Zig Ziglar

The Oxford Dictionary defines the word Realization as 'The **Achievement** of something **Desired** or **Anticipated**.'

The BENEFITS of this state are:
If we are able to reach the final developmental stage of Realization, we can be proud of ourselves because we have become the best possible

version of ourselves. And to stay at the peak of our own self we have to renew ourselves on an ongoing relentless basis to avoid stagnation. As I mentioned earlier on in the book, ultimate lack of motion is death.

Realization can come in many forms to us. It might be
- that a relationship requires constant fruitful communication between partners for it to work.
- that your health requires never-ending care which could involve dietitians, personal trainers, physiotherapists, etc.
- realizing that your children not only need you to grow up but just as importantly their extended family like grandparents, uncles, cousins and also their peers.
- the ultimate realization that you cannot achieve happiness just by being independent. It is even more important to be interdependent which means being able to communicate in the right way with other people.

As you can see realization lived at its best is almost like experiencing a miracle, one that you have created yourself. Unfortunately, there is again the possibility of failure when we are already so close to the finish line of our divine being.

Again, we speak of the dysfunctional realization which works to our disadvantage and the functional realization which works in our favour.

DYSFUNCTIONAL REALIZATION	FUNCTIONAL REALIZATION
You think that your way is the only way to go without listening to your partner.	You ask your partner for his opinion on the project you have in mind.
Your child struggles at school and you disregard the teacher's offer of a tutor.	You are grateful for the teacher's suggestion and thankful for the possibility of a tutor.
You are planning a family holiday without asking the other family members for their input and wishes.	You discuss the holiday plans with your family and you all agree on a holiday where every member gets their share of fun activity they imagine and want for themselves.

DYSFUNCTIONAL REALIZATION	FUNCTIONAL REALIZATION
In the case of my girlfriend, she did not want to drive the car for months after a car accident.	The functional way to deal with her situation would have been to realize that with her husband's help she would have been confident behind the steering wheel in no time at all.

So, after giving you a few examples on how things play out, I would like to help you in the process of turning a dysfunctional realization into a functional one:

1. Ask others for help.
2. Ask them for their opinion or input.
3. Show gratitude.

If you think that it all ends here, you are wrong. Yes, you are right, you have reached the ceiling, but it is a glass ceiling with more beyond it. Remember, to be happy you never want to stagnate, so if you have reached the point of Functional Realization in one area of your life you must keep looking for a new challenge where you will start back with Reliance again which then requires you to move through the steps of all four stages in just the same way.

"YOU NEVER STOP LEARNING."

Imagine you're entering a new relationship and you have all that knowledge. What a difference will that make!

In my case, the model works backwards.

I was in **Realization** when I met my husband. I made myself depend on him financially and emotionally and plummeted back into **Reliance** with loving him unconditionally.

I stayed there for a long time and slowly started to rebel. First, I was in **Dysfunctional Rebellion** and played the blame game until I decided to do something about it and realized the only person who could help me was myself. That is when I found myself in **Functional Rebellion**. I was sick and tired of being stuck in that life.

If I had waited for a change, I would have been stuck in **Dysfunctional Results,** but I put a plan for leaving into action and achieved **Functional Results**. If I had tried to achieve the last state all by myself, I would have been in **Dysfunctional Realization** but I chose to accept the help of friends and therefore achieved **Functional Realization**.

I reached what I thought was the ceiling, yet it was only a glass ceiling with more beyond it.

So, listen carefully now and pay attention:

The **Ultimate Realization** is that happiness can only come if we are in love with ourselves. I was not that young anymore but I got there eventually and the most important thing now for me is **"I am in love with myself"**.

♦ Abundance ♦
Spread your Wings

As always, I am inviting you to find a quiet space.
Light a candle.
Listen to soft music.
Or go for a walk through Mother Nature. After coming back from your peaceful walk, try and brainstorm your situation and assess at what level of developmental stage you are.

_____
_____
_____

If you are reliant, write down in which areas of your life you rely on somebody.

_____
_____
_____
_____

How can you undo your reliance?
What would it take and how would that change your life in the future?

_____
_____
_____

It would then bring you to the next level of development. You then start to rebel to the current situation.

To change your situation, you want to be in the state of Functional Rebellion.

But be careful because as soon as you start blaming somebody else for your situation, you are in Rebellion but in Dysfunctional Rebellion which will not change your future for the better. You will then forever play the blame game.

You need to realize that you are the only person in the whole universe who can help yourself.

So, think about and write down, what you need to do to change your current situation.

What are the action steps that you are going to follow through to make a change? (One step at a time)

_____

_____

_____

_____

That is how you know you are on the right track and then you will move up to the next Developmental Level, which is Results.

You know now that it is up to you to change your future, so make yourself accountable and check in with yourself if you are on track with your action-taking. Be aware that sometimes it takes the help of others to achieve your results. That is totally okay and normal.

Who is or are the people, who I need to help me to grow on my journey?

_____

_____

_____

In fact, it is this awareness that will allow you to move up to the next level which is Realization. You think you are satisfied in having achieved your results but in reality, you are seeking for the next challenge.

What will be my next challenge?

_____
_____
_____
_____

This cycle is unique to human nature, because as human beings we constantly seek to evolve. We cannot stagnate, we must always move forward. And in trying to accomplish your next challenge, you will fall back into the Reliant Level again because you start the learning curve from the bottom end upwards again.

Now you have the awareness of how to evolve as an individual and how to reach the next level of thinking.

I trust you will have fun in playing with this model and remember, most importantly:

LOVE YOURSELF

Chapter Six
Stay True to Yourself Always

"Stay true to yourself, yet always be open to learn.
Work hard, and never give up on your dreams,
Even when nobody else believes they come true but you.
These are not clichés but real tools you need
No matter what you do in life
To stay focused on your path."

By Phillip Sweet

♥ AWARENESS ♥

The very title of this chapter was an immensely valuable and important lesson in my life because there was a time when I did not stay true to myself and followed someone else's truth and values. And that was exactly the reason for the rather dark, not-so-fulfilling and happy moments of my existence. My life could have looked very differently to what it turned out to be, had I lived by what was of value and significance to me.

And that is why I want to make you, my dear reader, aware of what can happen if you don't stay true to yourself. So, let me refer to how I experienced it.

As mentioned earlier on, life was amazingly good for me growing up. It was really planned out and just the way I wanted it and most importantly, I was aware of what I wanted my life to look like. I could see myself as a successful, well-respected business woman travelling the world.

I was very happy and content with what I had already achieved. After finishing my schooling successfully, I was looking after myself. My health and fitness played a big role and I started to jog and went to the gym to keep my body that way. Plus, I developed reasonable and healthy eating habits and felt on top of the game.

So, in general I felt good and I looked good and that's also how other people perceived me.

I liked going out having a lot of fun and had good friends I could share all that with. I always managed to get a very satisfying job, yet after being in a job for a year or two, I felt like there was more and I was never afraid to look for another job and start a new, better paid position. So, I always gave it a go, applied for the next job and usually got it because at that time I was living congruently with my values which were first and foremost independence and freedom.

Speaking about values, I would like to share my hierarchy of values, the way it was for me at that time:

Independence and Freedom, I valued most.
Career and Personal Growth was almost just as important as Independence and Freedom
Health and Fitness
Fun
Security
Love

Love was placed right at the bottom of the list, not by mistake but because who needs love if you are happy the way you are. Let's just have fun instead. And so, everything was going the way I wanted it, and whenever I had to make a decision, I instantly knew which way I had to go. That was the single me, responsible only for myself.

And then I met my husband. That was the big game changer in my life. I am not saying that I regret meeting him, not at all because we had a wonderful life with two beautiful children together, of which one of them, my daughter, gave me my sweet darling of a grand-daughter. Only, I did not have the knowledge back then, that I do have now. I could have saved our family many heart aches, I believe.

And that is the valuable message that I would like to pass on to you, my sister-reader. I would like you to be wiser in making decisions than I have been. So, please do take my advice to heart and listen, rather read carefully to what follows.

In the moment of meeting my husband, I experienced something that I would have never thought to be possible, especially for me, that independent and freedom-loving girl who loved fun, excitement, adventure, and meeting lots of people.

It was love, deep and endless, true love. And it hit me like a lightning bolt. That feeling presented itself in a way I had never known anything like it before meeting him.

What happened next, was a total shake up of my stable, and yet freedom loving, adventurous existence. Let me tell you that the hierarchy of my values was tipped upside down in a mere instant. In an instance, love was tremendously important to me and moved from the bottom of the list, right to the top. And because of that deep love, I made the mistake of giving myself up, I committed totally and entirely to him and his life. One could think that this is exactly how it should be when you are in love with somebody.

But let me tell you, by doing so, I ended up accepting his values to be also my values in the order they were important to him which wasn't really congruently to how I wanted it to be or how it used to be in my life originally – as I shared with you earlier on. So, what had happened was, that my values suddenly got totally shaken up and put out of proportion to my core needs.

I did not look after myself in such a careful way anymore, my fitness level decreased massively and it wasn't that important for me to do my regular jogs anymore. I quit my gym membership because instead, I preferred to spend all my spare time with my new lover.

CHAINS OFF - WINGS ON

Even the rest of my values moved to different positions. Some values were replaced by new ones and did not count anymore at all. I still had a very good job at the time, but it was not the most important thing anymore as I no longer had to finance a place to live in by myself. We moved in together and shared everything, so the pressure on me to look after everything financially myself disappeared and with it did my independence – not from one day to another, but it vanished slowly along the progression of our relationship.

Can you see how my values turned around? For as long as we had no children, some of our values were the same and of equal importance. For example, we still shared the fun of going out, turning sometimes days to nights and vice versa due to my partner working late nights as a restaurateur. On weekends especially, we could only think of going out after midnight which meant no night sleep. And too often, we both went to work the next day without sleeping at all. So, the fun part was still part of our lives at that stage.

Giving birth to our first child, the value of having fun in going out together got replaced by another one that I had never considered before, and that was the value of caring. Being responsible and looking after another helpless little human being. All mothers know what that means for ourselves, we, or our husbands are no longer the number one to give our full attention to.

So, let's recap of what was happening to my perfectly-balanced life and my congruent values. When I was by myself living in accordance with my values, I was the only person I had to care for. The moment, I met my partner - we only got married after our daughter was one and a half years old – and then became a mother who had to care for two other people than for herself, the tables had changed.

Let me share with you that I was taught the hard way, how to no longer care for myself but for another human in a very intense way because our daughter was born with an anomaly which meant she was taken off me, the instance she was born. I got to cuddle her for a brief moment on my belly straight after popping out but then she was sent to another hospital for instant surgery (as I shared with you earlier on).

Can you imagine what effect that had on the hierarchy of my existing values?

I did not think about myself at all and my ego did not matter anymore neither. All that counted was my sick child to overcome her problems, survive them and to be able to live and have a normal life. Immediately all my values went down the drain and the only one, most important thing to me was my child. The one thing that was going through my mind at that time, was the question why it was not me, who could have been inflicted with problems during the pregnancy. On the contrary, I had the most delightful pregnancy you can imagine. It suited me, I bloomed and carrying and feeling my child inside me was such a joy for me. So why, was it that my child had to suffer?

Of course, I did not come up with any answers – how could I?

And it was because of this certain realization that I disregarded my own values even more. I was under the impression that the only one aspect of my life I had to focus on from now on, was my daughter, my own flesh and blood. I would do anything to help her overcome her challenges to be able to grow into a healthy and happy young woman.

Of course, it was painful to see my child in pain and yet I couldn't do anything about it but have faith into the doctors who looked after her. I just had to deal with it. So, the focus on my career at that stage was totally gone, it was non-existent. My personal growth was only there as a mother. The only way I would work on myself, was to become the mother my sick child needed, other than that I didn't work on myself anymore. All that mattered to me was being a good mother.

Let's have a quick look to where my old values had gone and what the hierarchy of my new values looked like:

Caring was number one, caring for my sick child, for my partner and serving my partner. Security was just as important to be able to care for what was important to me.

Yet, where were independence, freedom, career, and success now? Can you see how they got even removed from my vocabulary? And all of these new values like Caring, Serving, Security appearing that I did not even know the slightest of when I was single.

So, you can imagine what happened next. I was no longer living in harmony with my personal values at all and what occurred to me was, that I got confused.

So, there it is, I'd like to ask you my dear sister at this point, if you can see how important it is to stay true to yourself and live by your values. Can you see that without you realizing, something can change, just because you listen to the one you love and at the same time ignore the screams for help from your own soul?

For as long as I was true to myself and lived according to my values, I was a very happy, striving person. I was still content and not aware of any change in the beginning of my relationship. It is over time when your dissatisfaction rises from within you because you are ignoring your very own needs. So, I am asking you now, doesn't it make total sense to stay true to yourself and therefore live in harmony with your inner self? Isn't it true that you can achieve anything, no matter what other people think of you or tell you to do?

This is the only way for you to take charge of your life and stay happy whether as a single or in a relationship. And by doing just that, you then control the outcome of your life which brings you happiness and fulfillment, not only for you but also for you and your partner and the people around you, and most importantly for your children.

The other side to the coin though is, imagine what happens if you don't stay true to yourself and to your values? The moment you arrive at a crossroad, all of a sudden you start getting so confused. You won't know which direction to turn to because on the one hand, your inner values tell you to go in one direction whereas the other values that you have adapted from your partner or other outside factors make you go against your direction, and as result will cause you an inner conflict. It is okay to live with an inner conflict on hands for a short period of time, but you do not want to leave it too long to get things right because your core you will suffer from that issue dramatically. – Listen to somebody who has been there and done that. - If you continue to battle these inner fights, it gets very tiring and in the end, you realize that you cannot keep going like that because it consumes you. On top of being unhappy, worn out and tired, you will lose yourself, the person who you have been and who you are meant to be all along and for the rest of your being.

And that is exactly what happened with me. After 20 years of denying my own values, I saw myself at a point where I couldn't keep going any longer. I would have gotten sick because the person I used to be did not exist anymore at all, neither on the inside nor on the outside. Of course, deep inside, but forgotten and not cared for in the very core, there was still a spark of the adventurous, igniting flame that used to be me. I was still somewhere but I couldn't find myself anymore. I couldn't dig that person out because my true self was fully engulfed with someone else's values, the ones that I have been living with through my marriage and my children. But they were not mine and therefore, I somehow had lost my true identity, the person that I was meant to be.

I am certain that you are able to see the importance by now of finding out what your core values really are.

Now pay attention, it does not finish here. In terms of relationships, it is indispensable to determine your and your partner's values and communicate them to each other, and also give them grading as to what are the more important ones and the least necessary ones to follow. For a co-existence to be happy, long-lasting and fulfilled you want to make sure that you find common ground in most of your values, or even better work out the values that will be of importance for the two of you and then also decide together on their significance.

So, what I am saying here is that communication is the non-plus ultra in every relationship, whether it be of intimate kind or business related.

The magic behind it all, is the following:

Know your and your partner's values, communicate them to each other and don't forget to establish values that concern you both, like values around the upbringing of your children, values around the house, as simple as values around how clean you want your house to be or how important it is to keep the house and its surroundings clean and tidy. There is a lot to think about when it comes to living together because you both are individuals with individual needs who at one point are going to share everything with each other without the loss of your individuality and your uniqueness. And not to forget, the significance of understanding each other's love language. Talk about your preferences and things you do not appreciate too much. Again, the need for communication arises for better understanding your partner's needs, dreams and not to forget fears.

And then try and have your common values match as much as possible, live both congruently by them and share a joyful, blessed and untroubled, wonderful co-existence. Then your everyday life will seem like a breeze. Everything will sort of fall into place and work itself out. Decisions that need to be made, will be taken like a no brainer. You will be filled with and radiate positive emotions like love, joy, optimism, certainty, and a hunger to live and you will be contagious to everyone around you. People will look at you in dismay and wonder how you are pulling such a wonderful live in perfect harmony off with your dear other half. Only you know the secret and will find pleasure in sharing the magic trick with everyone else who is in need of it.

Yet, unfortunately there is always the chance that you do not get it right. You either do not pay enough attention to your and your partner's values or you do not give them enough significance.

Because of that neglect a disaccord might arise, creating a gap between the two of you and it will grow until the situation becomes unbearable and ultimately the only way out, is for one of you to leave. Negative and uncomfortable emotions like doubt, fear, guilt, confusion, and frustration - just to name a few – will determine your very existence.

I love a quote Anthony Robbins refers to in his book "Awaken the Giant Within", it is a quote from Joseph Wood Krutch who says,

"Every time a Value is born,
Existence takes a new meaning;
Every time one dies, some part of that meaning passes away."

♣ APPROACH ♣
Because what it comes down to is your **VALUES** that absolutely determine the direction of your life.

Anthony Robbins describes values as the 'Magnetic Pull' that control our lives. They are sort of a compass that give you the direction in which you want to go. And they absolutely influence whether you are content and joyous or not.

As I continue to talk about values, I would like to make you aware of the fact that we subdivide values into the following:

"Ends and Means Values":
For example, your values are success and money. In that case, success is your ends value, it is what you want to experience in the end. Money, on the other hand, is the means value, it gives you the feeling of having success.

"Moving Towards and Moving Away Values":
Moving Towards Values are all the emotions we want to feel, all the ones that make us feel good. For example, love, happiness, integrity, etc.

Moving Away Values are all the values we want to rather avoid, for example rejection, anger, frustration, etc. They represent all the negative aspects of our lives.

And then there are **"Rules"** around values which can either enhance our existence or put us through a lot of pain, depending on what rules you choose to make.

For example, you might tell yourself that you can only be loved if you earn that love. In that case you are telling yourself that you need to work hard to be worthy of that love. Can you see what pressure that puts onto that love and yourself? With such tough rules you are restricting yourself big time. Saying it out loud even feels like a knot in your stomach, isn't it?

Wouldn't you rather have softer, kinder rules?

For example, instead of saying that you had to earn the love, wouldn't it be much kinder for yourself to say something like, "I am loved because I am a beautiful being who deserves to be loved."

That was just a brief introduction to the different kinds of values and their rules, all of which I will be explaining in more detail in the section down below.

So, please stay focused and keep reading on.

♠ ACTIONS ♠

Jim Rohn says,
"The major value in life is not what you get.
The major value in life is what you become."

According to the Cambridge Dictionary, Values are 'the **Principles** that help you to decide what is **right** and **wrong**, and how to act in various situations.'

In the world of coaching:
– Values are everything we think is important to us.
– the emotional states that we want to experience,
– the force in front of us that impacts our decisions and
– ultimately our values shape our destiny.
– They are like a compass for our lives.
– How do we know what our values are and how do we know if we live our life congruently with our values?
– Living according to your values makes you happy.
– Doing the opposite and not living by the values you honour in your life, creates confusion. You struggle in making decisions.

LIVING CONGRUENTLY W/VALUES	NOT LIVING CONGRUENTLY W/VALUES
A woman is successful in business. Then she falls pregnant. She always wanted a family and that is one of her most important values, she is happy about the pregnancy and the fact that she is going to be a mother.	If that same woman never really wanted children and her value number one is success and recognition in her career, then she won't be so happy about the pregnancy and she might even think about abortion. She sees herself in a debacle of decision making which can cause pain as bad a depression.

No need to look at such life changing examples to look at values. Imagine you are invited to a party with your partner. You are very excited because socializing, having fun and being in crowds is one of your favourite things to do. So, you are shining on that night and enjoying yourself to the fullest.	Your partner on the other hand, is not very social and detests crowds and small talk and would rather fully emerge himself in the book he is reading at the moment. He only comes along to make you feel happy. He might be bored though, not interacting much with people and all he can think of is going home. His values lie at home in the peace and quiet space where he can read his book. By coming along, his values are not met and therefore he is not happy.

Can you see the important role of values and their congruency?

In conclusion to this part of the chapter, I am sure you can see the importance of knowing your values. If you are living congruently with your values, making a decision is easy. Whereas, every time you struggle in knowing which direction to go, you are not clear what your values are, and you are not living according to them. AND you don't know what is most important in your life and therefore experience PAIN.

At the end of this chapter there is an exercise on how to find out your values.

We distinguish two types of values, **ENDS and MEANS VALUES.**

"The value of life is not in its duration,
but in its donation.
You are not important because of how long you live,
you are important because of how effective you live."

by Myles Munroe

ENDS VALUES:
An Ends Value is the Emotional state you desire.
Examples for Ends Values are:

– Love, Happiness, Joy, Freedom, Independence, Fulfilment,
= Everything to do with feelings

MEANS VALUES:

A Means Value is everything that contributes to giving you a certain feeling.

Examples for Means Values are:
Money, Success in your job, Family, Children
All these values are means for you to trigger the emotional states you desire.

Let me bring it together in an example:
If I asked you, "What does family give you?" and you answered "It makes me happy,
I feel loved and it gives me a sense of security."

Family is purely the means, the reason for you to achieve Happiness, Love and Security.

The Ends Values are Happiness, Love and Security.

It is the Ends Values that activate the set of emotions we are after.

Many people are not clear about the difference.

For their whole life they chase the Means Values which causes them pain, for they are not fulfilled leading to confusion.

Emotions are in the Ends Values. They make us experience fulfilling our purpose.

And then there are **MOVING TOWARDS VALUES** and **MOVING AWAY VALUES:**

MOVING TOWARDS VALUES:

"Joy, feeling one's own value,
being appreciated and loved by others,
feeling useful and capable of production
are all factors of enormous value for the human soul."

by Maria Montessori

They are all the values we link the most pleasure within our life. They are the desirable state of emotions like Love, Success, Freedom, Independence, Fun, Health, Power, Excitement, Happiness, Integrity, etc. That is what we look to achieve ultimately.

MOVING AWAY VALUES:

"I have always believed, and I still believe,
that whatever good or bad fortune may come our way
we can always give it meaning and transform it into something of value."

by Hermann Hesse

They are the emotional states we try to avoid like Fear, Anger, Frustration, Rejection, Depression, Failure, Guilt, Humiliation, Loneliness, etc.

Now looking at the fact that we all have our lists with values that we link pleasure to and on the other hand, the list we link pain to, we might see ourselves in a predicament because when we look at both hierarchies of values that we want to achieve and on the opposite side the ones we try to avoid, we might self-sabotage ourselves and set ourselves up for pain.

Let me explain:
Down below find two hierarchies of values

Moving Towards	Moving Away
Family	Confrontation
Love	Loneliness
Success	Frustration
Comfort	Insecurity

Can you see how this person is setting herself up for failure?
Her no. 1 Moving Towards Value = Family
Her no. 1 Moving Away Value = Confrontation

Do you know of any family where there are never arguments and confrontation happening? In this case we speak of a conflict in Values.

So, later on when establishing your lists with values that empower and disempower you, be careful that they are not contradictive to avoid unnecessary suffering.

One other possibility of causing agony even when we live congruently with our values, can be caused by **THE RULES** we make about what needs to happen to feel good or the opposite.

RULES:

"The golden rule is that
there are no rules."

by George Bernard Shaw

The **Collins English Dictionary** says that **Rules** are **Instructions** that tell you what you are allowed to do and what you are not allowed to do.

Anthony Robbins discovered that Rules are a shortcut for our brains. They help us to have a sense of certainty about the consequences of our actions. Who do you think is telling us what we are allowed to feel and when to feel good or bad or anything at all?

Yes, you guessed right: It is always us telling ourselves what needs to happen to feel loved, or to feel that we have achieved something or what need to be the circumstances for us to feel secure and safe.

By doing so, we sabotage our values again. Like so much in life, rules can empower us or lead us to massive pain and confusion. To avoid that from happening, we need to be very careful with how to language our rules and how we link them to our Moving Towards and Moving Away Values.

Let me show you in examples how rules can have a positive and a negative impact on our values:

MOVING TOWARDS VALUES

EMPOWERING RULES	DIS-EMPOWERING RULES
FAMILY I feel happy about my family because I acknowledge to myself that I have brought up my children to my best ability.	I only feel happy about my family if in comparison with other families I can see my children stand out.
LOVE To feel love, I allow myself to give love and to receive it at the same time in a grateful way.	To feel loved, I need to feel as if I have worked hard to earn to be loved.
SUCCESS I acknowledge my achievements because I know I was committed to doing the best I could.	To see myself successful I need to be admired by others.

MOVING AWAY VALUES

EMPOWERING RUES	DIS-EMPOWERING RULES
CONFRONTATION It is okay to have arguments in a relationship, we are all allowed to voice our opinion. To understand better I will listen more carefully in future.	I don't like arguing because I feel as if I am never understood.
LONELINESS I am fine with being lonely because I know I can concentrate on myself and actually look after myself for a change.	I can't stand loneliness because I feel as if other people are avoiding me.
FRUSTRATION When I feel frustrated I tell myself to be more patient with myself and others and try to understand them or the situation better.	I don't like the feeling of being frustrated. I makes me feel depressed.

The above examples show how easy it is to give in and just feel bad. The secret though lies in trying to flip the coin and do everything in your ability to feel good, even if it takes a big deal of an effort. The reward is priceless.

"Change your Values, Change your Life", by Anthony Robbins in "Awaken the Giant Within".

That's how simple it is. Commit to thinking about your values and making the necessary change to achieve your full potential.

In the "Spread Your Wings" Section, you will find all the valuable exercises to put you and your values on the right track. According to Anthony Robbins, people will do more to avoid pain than to achieve pleasure.

So be careful to head into the right direction.

♦ Abundance ♦

I hope that in the meantime you had a few aha moments. Moments when you realized why certain problems in your relationship exist.

Spread your Wings

Find a quiet space, light a candle, listen to soft music and take time out to get clear on your values and rules and go through the following exercise:

First and foremost, you want to find out your values. You are able to do this by asking yourself:

"What is the most important thing in your life?"

Then follow the steps below:

1. Step - Hierarchy of Values: Create a list of values and rank them according to how important they are to you on a scale from 1 to 10.

_____
_____
_____
_____
_____

2. Step - Ask yourself and write it down if you live by each and every one of your values.

3. Step - Be clear about the change that you are looking for and rank your values in the according new order and delete some existing values if they do not serve you and add new values if you think they serve your purpose. Ask yourself what the new values need to be in order for you to reach your desire and destiny.

_____

_____

_____

_____

_____

_____

4. Step - Remember: "Change your values and Change your life." That's how powerful values are and we are not our values. We are much more than our values.

5. Step - Now condition yourself to use these new acquired values as your compass and live by them, otherwise they just remain empty words on a piece of paper.

6. Step - Then think about your rules and realign them with your values. Once you are clear about your rules, communicate them with your partner.

Then answer the following questions as precisely as you can:
What does it take for you to feel loved by your husband, children or other important people in your life?
What does it take for you to feel confident?
What does it take for you to feel understood?
What does it take for you to feel independent within your relations?

STAY TRUE TO YOURSELF ALWAYS

_____

_____

_____

_____

_____

_____

_____

Chapter Seven
Pulling on One String

"What we plant in the soil of contemplation, we shall reap in the harvest of action."

by Meister Eckhart

♥ AWARENESS ♥

As I shared with you earlier on, the way things work out the best is, that you are in line with your partner, and therefore also share the same beliefs, dreams and visions.

Let me explain to you what I mean by this and then talk about beliefs in general and how they can and are going to influence the future we are creating for ourselves and our immediate environment.

When my partner and I met, it was an immediate agreement between us that one day we would venture out and explore another country, not just for sightseeing and holidaying but in fact to build up a new existence for us and our family to be.

This very promise that we made each other started to come alive when my mother planned a vacation to Australia with a group of friends. Seeing her disembark to the far away country hardly known and heard of, ignited a thought pattern in both of us which made us investigate this unfamiliar territory closely. As you can only learn so much about another country from the internet, television and books, we decided to get a feeling of the country Australia from first hand by travelling there and seeing and experiencing for ourselves. So, we followed my mum's footsteps and booked a vacation of three weeks to check out the East Coast of Australia.

Needless to say what followed, we went through the visa application process and everything that was involved and eight months later it was time to pack up our entire life into a 12 foot shipping container and saw ourselves with our six and a half-year-old daughter and eight months old son with just a few suit cases on a plane with end destination Sydney/Australia where we did not know a soul. It was just the four of us with the few belongings that fitted into our luggage.

Looking back at that time and talking about it, makes all the countless challenges, heart aches and tears that came along with it, appear so distant and indifferent, almost as if they never existed. But, trust me, they were for real and that was just the very beginning of it all.

And I am certain that every single expat amongst you knows exactly what I am talking about, as you all have gone through the whole experience yourselves, partly exciting like an adventure, partly daunting like a drama and certainly partly filled with sadness because of leaving everything and everybody you loved, behind you. Of course, the impressions vary for each and everyone but the core issues and confrontations are always the same.

And what do you think it is, we all have in common?

Yes, you are right, we all share the same belief that we would be able to follow through with the process, no matter how tough the goings would be or become. We shared the belief that we can do it because we all had a big enough reason WHY we wanted to embark on the adventure of shifting our existence into a foreign territory. For some of us, it was love that made us go live in the distance, for others it was political issues and for some it was pure adventure or the thought of a better and brighter future for their family that got us here.

So, let me get back to share a little more about my new beginnings here in Australia because as mentioned before, nothing fell into place for us and our endurance got tested more than just once or twice.

As we were granted to come to Australia on a business visa, we had to own and run a business – in our case a business in the hospitality industry, i.e. some kind of coffee shop or restaurant, following certain criteria.

That is where the next set of challenges arose:

At the time, businesses were not required to register for GST which also meant that they were not required to keep any documents about the everyday turnover or takings which made it kind of hard to put a purchase price on a restaurant that you were willing to pay. Because too often the sale price that business owners asked for was outrageous and did not match the value of their income anywhere near. So, it was very important, to watch businesses you were interested to buy over a certain time to see for yourself if the asking price was justified.

After a few months doing just that we decided to buy our first business in Australia, a very busy coffee shop on an upmarket street in Brisbane, opposite a movie theatre. We employed around fifteen staff and worked in two shifts from 6 am until 12 midnight or even later seven days a week. My husband was at the coffee shop for almost the entire opening hours while I looked after the children, learning how to do the book keeping with MYOB, baking the desserts and organizing all the rest that needed to be done. And on top of everything else, we only had one car at the time which meant I had to drive my husband early mornings to work and then go and pick him up again late when he had finished.

As you can imagine, running a business 24/7 without getting any spare time was not sustainable over a longer period of time and we had to face the facts that we would have to sell and look for a more doable way of how to conducting business so that we could also be there for our children as we did not have and still do not have any family here with us.

At this point, one could think that we were failing big time and I must admit that we had our doubts about being able to make a living here in our new far away home, but we were determined to give it another shot as we still shared the belief of succeeding.

We came up with the idea of running a farm of some sort which would enable us to work from home. But neither my husband nor myself come from a farming back ground and after looking into flower farms, been sprout farms, rhubarb farms, olive farms, mushroom farms, etc. we decided that it would be too risky to go into business as we had no knowledge whatsoever about how to run a farm.

We saw our beliefs of successfully running a business here in Australia and establishing a new beginning challenged yet again.

But we were still not ready to give up because in our mind's eye we could still see the end goal of us bringing up our children in this adopted home of ours.

In the end, we found an empty tenancy in an older shopping centre with low weekly rent and decided to establish a Mediterranean restaurant from scratch. It was just an empty space, but we could visualize where the kitchen, the pizza oven, the bar and the dining area would be in an instant. We got in touch with a builder because we needed to put in a wall to separate the kitchen from the bar and the dining area, hired a hydraulic engineer to set the restaurant up according to Council's regulations and painted the walls and tiled the floors ourselves. These were exiting times and we could see our dream of owning our very own restaurant become a reality.

Three months into trading and just starting to make ourselves noticed by locals, we got the bad news that our first business visa was about to expire and that there was no possibility of being granted an extension as we had not been trading long enough to have met the necessary requirements.

Any idea, how hard that hit us and what that meant?

Well, to say the least, we were devastated and yet again tested if we would endure and have the strength to continue.

Remember the talk about our beliefs? Yes, even in that depressing moment, us too, we remembered what we believed in and yet again we stood up to our challenge and fought for what we knew, was our goal.

We got sent offshore to apply for a second business visa which we were told originally would never be granted within a week – that was the time that we had planned in for our trip to Fiji and it was as long as we could allow to be away from our restaurant that had just opened the doors to the public three months prior to the devastating news.

With perseverance, persuasion and a lot of phone calls between our lawyer and the Australian High Commission in Suva, we succeeded in returning with our second business visa being granted, which allowed us, not only to stay in Australia but also to continue running our Mediterranean restaurant which we would own and run, well known to locals and beyond for another seven years before selling.

It was also the reason that only a year into running it, we met all the requirements that were needed to be granted our Permanent Residency.

Now, let me ask you this: Do you think that our beliefs had served us well and that it was worth holding on to them?

♣ APPROACH ♣

BELIEFS
So, let's talk about beliefs and know that they are not the same for everyone, because we all give different meanings to either words, thoughts or even experiences that we had. In the language of experts, we are talking about us having different Maps and 'The Map is not the Territory'. And all the information and experiences that our mind gathers, is passed through filters, **three filters** in total, called **Generalisation, Distortion** and **Deletion**.

Let me explain all of that in the following pages because I can imagine how you feel right now. It seems to you as if you were just opening a Chinese Dictionary because none of the above makes any sense to you.

- A belief is a possibility filter.
- It is a feeling of certainty about something.
- It is our beliefs that create and shape our reality.
- Beliefs have the power to create and the power to destroy.

- They can serve and empower us or limit or even destroy our full potential.
- They can be the reason for us not reaching our goals.
- Because we tend to generalize, distort and delete information.
- The beliefs of different people most likely also mean different things to each and every one because we all have different maps of the world.
- My map is not your map and also 'The Map is not the Territory'.

♠ ACTIONS ♠

Beliefs

"I can believe things that are true and
things that aren't true and I can believe
things where nobody knows if they are true or not."

Unknown

According to the Cambridge Dictionary a **Belief** is 'the feeling of being certain that something exists or is true.'

The building block of a belief is an idea. For example, if I say, "I am hot" (as in sexy):

Hot is the idea. Now think of the idea as a table top without legs yet. How can you say, you are sexy?

Because you have **references** to support the idea. And therefore the references become the legs to your table top, which might be:

- "I have an awesome figure."
- "I have long, wavy hair."
- "I wear tight clothes."
- "I have big, full breasts."

Now your idea has the building blocks to form my belief, why you think you are sexy.

The references are formed by our own experiences or through information from other people or purely through our imagination. The most powerful references come from our personal experiences because of the emotions attached to them.

Beliefs can be very empowering:
- In my story, the beliefs that my husband and I shared were working for us. They were the reason for us to live in Australia today.
- It is the same if you go to a job interview and tell yourself that this is your chance. You are going to get that job because it is exactly suited for you. Because of that belief your physiology and language express a certainty around your self-esteem which radiates and can be sensed by others.
- Imagine yourself taking part in an obstacle course in a group with others. You all share the belief that you are going to accomplish the thirty odd challenges. And when you feel as if you have reached your limit, you will remember that you all believed in getting to the finish line, so you call upon your energy reserves and keep going until that finish line is crossed.

Beliefs can also be rather dis-empowering or limiting:
- If for example, a child grows up being told that he/she was not good enough for anything, then this very person will have problems as an adult achieving any goals because the limiting beliefs which were created back in their childhood, are holding them back.
- I have a dear girlfriend who decided to go for her driver's licence as an adult. Her husband told her that she should not be driving on the high way because that was too dangerous for her. – Now, do you think she is driving on the highway ten or twenty years later? Certainly not, because her belief is that it is not safe for her to do so. Her ego, like everybody else's ego, is protecting her and therefore holds her back from doing so.
- If your belief is that you cannot go for a run when it is raining because of getting wet, then you are less likely to do so.

So, having established what a belief is and how they influence us, let's have a look at this so-called 'Map'- and 'Territory' thing.

The Map is not the Territory:

"It's not the events in our lives that shape us, but our beliefs as to what those events mean."

by Anthony Robbins

One of the explanations of the meaning of the word '**Map**' in the Cambridge Dictionary is that it is 'the drawing that gives you a particular type of information about a particular area.'

With the word 'Map' we mean the Map of the world of a person. That is how each and every one of us sees every situation, every experience and the meaning of every single word according to their understanding. It is, therefore, subjective to that person's perception. The way we describe certain things is not the same reality for everybody. It is the reality we give it.

The Cambridge Dictionary describes the word 'Territory' as 'an area that an animal or person tries to control or thinks belongs to them.'

The Territory describes the surroundings of what is being described, it is objective and as a result, the same for everybody.

Let me give you an example to make it easier to understand:

- Your partner and you are invited to a friend's house. You describe the house as being messy because you are very meticulous. Your partner, on the other hand, describes it as being lovely. He doesn't mind objects lying around spread out everywhere.
So, the house is the Territory and the words 'messy' and 'lovely' are your and your partner's map.

Can you see, how we interpret the same situation with different meanings? The reason behind it is that we are all meaning-making machines.

Other examples would be:

- You might allow your daughter to wear a t-shirt with deeper V-neck because in the household where you were growing up that was

normal and therefore tolerated. Your partner though might have a different idea about that because of either coming from a different cultural background altogether or simply because in his family one would think you might be asking for trouble.
Territory = t-shirt, Map = V-neck

- Has it ever happened to you that you could not agree on a certain colour for something, you might have said dark green and the other person dark grey? Again because of our different experiences we have different beliefs about it.
Territory = the object, Map = dark green/dark grey

- You are going on a hike, standing in front of a climb. For you it might seem steep, for somebody else who is fitter it might seem easy.
Territory = the climb, Map = steep/easy

As you can already see that due to the different Maps we all have, dis-agreements, misunderstandings and arguments are very likely to happen if we use only our Map as a reference. And it so happens that there are some more reasons for such differences. → 'Thoughts'.

When we talk about our thoughts, we distinguish between thoughts in our Surface Structure and thoughts in our Deep Structure.

Our beliefs are formed in the Deep Structure. That is where we have specific thoughts, or specific beliefs whereas the Surface Structure is just the everyday talking. All our beliefs and thoughts are then hacked by **Generalization, Distortion** and **Deletion** because we are bombarded with two million bits of information per second. And we can only process 134 bits or 7 plus or minus 2 chunks of information.

Like I said earlier on, these three terms are the filters that our brain uses to only let that part of the information get through to us which is important to us. That part that falls into our 'Map'.

To make that easier to understand, let me explain how it works.

Generalization

"Two mysterious people live in my house.
Somebody and Nobody. Somebody did it
and Nobody knows who."

Unknown

The Cambridge Dictionary describes Generalization as 'a written or spoken statement in which you say or write that something is true all the time when it is true only some of the time.'

In the world of coaching, we say that generalization is when one particular experience is the reason for other experiences being classed the same way.

Some examples:
- "Everything always happens the same way."
- "Everybody thinks the same."
- "Nobody can tell me why."
- "All people are like that."

Can you see how we tend to generalize certain views on experiences? Another way of us dis-forming our thoughts is distortion.

Distortion

"The truth is not distorted here,
but rather a distortion is used
to get the truth."

by Flannery O'Connor

According to the Cambridge Dictionary 'to distort' means 'to change something so that it is false or wrong, or no longer means what it was intended to mean.'

In coaching, we talk about distortion as in being a change, a twist, or an exaggeration that makes something appear different from the way it really is.

Some examples:

- Can you remember the game Chinese Whisper we used to play as children, when we would stand in a circle? One child would say a word or sentence and pass it silently on to the next one and so on. The last person had to say out loud what was finally passed on to him. It was always rather funny because not once was the end result what was said in the beginning. The sentence always got twisted and had nothing to do with what the original sentence was. In other terms, the sentence got distorted.

- Another example in a relationship could be that somebody who grew up in a rather harsh unfriendly environment might see signs of kindness as something that the partner does because he wants something in return.

- Or you have been hurt having lived in a controlled relationship, you could then twist the caring kindness of a genuine, loving partner into the thought of being controlled yet again.

- Very interesting to mention here is the fact that procrastination is actually the ultimate distortion.

Wow, yet again, we twist and turn everything around, don't we? But that is not enough, some of the information we delete all together which brings us to the last modality of us influencing and changing what has been said.

Deletion

"More than once, I've wished my
real life had a delete key."

by Harlan Coben

The Cambridge Dictionary says that 'deletion is the process of removing something.'

In the context of coaching, it is our brain itself, removing information because it is considered unnecessary or the brain does not allow certain information reaching our conscious mind in the first place.

Some examples:

- Imagine you being part of a conversation and it is being said that the picnic is going to be held on a certain day at such and such place in sunny conditions only. You might have only heard the part with the date and the whereabout but not anymore the part where it said in 'sunny conditions' because your brain deleted that part of the conversation. As a result, you might turn up there on an overcast day and wonder why nobody is there.

- I am sure you all have been in situations where somebody told you about something, they were planning on doing and weeks later when they tell you about how much fun it was you say, "Hang on a moment, you did not tell me that!" You might have thought at the time that you are getting old and start to forget the one or other thing. In reality, your brain might have just removed that information because it did not seem important at the time.

- Children sometimes tell us about something that has happened at school but because it was not something that involved your child directly, your brain might delete the information and when other mums start talking about that incident, it seems to you that you have never heard about it before.

Are you getting the picture here, how easy it is to create misunderstandings if we just talk about ourselves without even thinking of or considering the other person?

In fact, can you imagine what difference that knowledge might make when you enter a new relationship?

Can you see the value in chunking down valuable information that has been given to you by your partner and what profound difference it can make whether or not to put all of the above into consideration when talking about re-occurring problems in the partnership?

♦ Abundance ♦
Spread your Wings

Find a quiet space,
light a candle and put on soft music or
go for a walk in nature and then do the following:

- Reflect on your life
- What beliefs do you hold?
- Do your beliefs serve you well?
- Look at the area of your life you are struggling with at the moment and find out the beliefs around this area. Obviously, they are not serving you well, so it's time to work out why.
- First find out what your beliefs are, write them down in the first half of the table below.
- What belief can you replace the current belief with that would change your life in a positive way? Write that new belief down in the second half of the table below, right opposite your old belief.

OLD BELIEFS	NEW BELIEFS

- Are you being held back in changing that belief because of secondary gain?
That means, do you hold the current belief to serve maybe your husband because of cultural differences or somebody else or simply because you know in the bottom of your heart that changing YOUR belief could cause discomfort?
- In that case, think about your and your partner's or that other person's Map of the World. Realizing that those two worlds might be two entirely different things, may help in understanding your partner or the other person better.
- If that is the case, you better ask yourself what serves you and only yourself best.
- We are responsible for leading an extraordinary life ourselves.
- Remember: It is YOU and ONLY YOU and YOUR BELIEFS that count.

Once you have found new beliefs to replace the old ones with, go a little deeper within yourself and find out what your Rules are or have been around your beliefs. If the Rules have been unkind to yourself and therefore not been serving you, try and replace them with ones that will be of advantage to you. Write the old unwanted rules down below into the table and put the new ones you want them to replace with in the opposite column.

OLD RULES	NEW RULES

Have fun with finding out Beliefs and Rules that serve you well and change your thinking around so that you can hold on to your beliefs, no matter how hard it will be and how many challenges you will have to face. If you find it hard to hold on to the newly-acquired thought pattern, then put your new Beliefs and Rules on sticky notes and put them on your bathroom mirror and on your fridge to be reminded of them all the time until you have adapted the new thought pattern automatically.

Because in the long run it is your happiness that counts! **Spread your wings!**

Chapter Eight
Love is Not Enough

"Our memories are our own,
and we cannot blame anything or anyone in the past
for any pain dwelling there.
If we open the door to them or
keep hashing over past incidents in our minds,
we have only ourselves to blame."

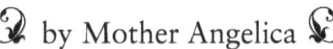 by Mother Angelica

♥ AWARENESS ♥

Why do I call my chapter "Love is not enough"?

I always thought that love is the one and only important thing for a person and in life in general to make a relationship work and to keep us happy. Unfortunately, I got taught the opposite because even after being separated or divorced from my husband now for over 10 years I still feel love for him in one way or another. It never disappeared entirely, nor did it ever transform into hatred.

So why did our relationship not work out, if the love was so strong that even after being apart and living different lives, there was still a fraction of it left? Let me share my story with you now.

I was very much in love with my husband when we first met, one could say – and he would be right – that I was enchanted, and so was he.

This strong feeling of affection was not only present when we first met but for all the years that we have been together, even at times when

I could not stand living under the same roof with him. He was the love of my life and I would do anything to keep that feeling alive and our co-existence intact.

His troubled past was familiar to me. I knew that he had left home when he was nineteen knowing that most likely he would never be able to return to his home country. Even though he knew he wouldn't be able to see his parents ever again, he jumped on a plane together with a friend, not even knowing where it would take them. That is how he arrived in Vienna, the capital of Austria as an asylum seeker.

Although he was enrolled at University to study economics back home, he was aware of his new circumstances which would lead him to accept any kind of work to be able to stay in that foreign country with different language that granted him asylum. And he was determined to make this work. His first jobs were tough and very labor-intensive and only with persistence, perseverance and putting all the savings aside, he was soon able to buy into a business with a friend and turned out to be a successful, self-made businessman.

Knowing that story about his past and how he was able to turn his situation around from being an asylum seeker to becoming a successful business man, I could not do anything but admire him for his hard work, his achievements and endurance. These were all the traits in him that made me love him even more, I guess. Besides the love, there was adoration and admiration and a bit of mystic around his origin, coming from an Arabian country. Here was I, a young woman who had the best childhood she could have ever asked for, protected throughout the years of growing up with no hardship to overcome at all, probably even naïve. Meeting this man who had to overcome so many obstacles so early in his life was my very first encounter with the eventuality that life could be a real bitch and that I had to count my blessings about how lucky I was, being born into such a healthy, loving and caring family.

As a note on the side, my – now ex-husband – never got to see his parents again after leaving them at age nineteen which is very sad, and most likely something he could never put behind him.

There was a political reason which made it impossible to ever return to his birth country and he knew he might have to pay with his life if he ever returned.

So, there was always this fear in him of being found out which of course determined not only his past but his whole existence. So, you could easily say that he had quite a troubled past and I felt for him in that respect, and therefore was determined to help him. As I would find out later on in life, I have always been the type of the rescuer, the person who could not see anybody suffer and who would always try to step in and help.

Coming back to the time when we met, he had a nine-year old daughter from his first marriage. And the way he presented himself to me and how I perceived him, he was a very caring and loving father who did everything in his power to be there for his daughter even though he was a fulltime business man, owning and running three restaurants in three different cities at the same time.

He had managers in two where he would just oversee the day-to-day business, and the main restaurant he ran himself from paperwork to prepping, cooking and looking after customers. Life was busy and full on for him.

However, he spoiled me a lot and adored me. We were unbelievably happy in our relationship and enjoyed every moment we were able to spend together up until we had our daughter. From the moment I became a mother, something changed. He started to become very controlling of me and he also couldn't accept the fact that our daughter was sick. He couldn't accept the fact that she had an anomaly, and so my life changed in an instant from experiencing only joy in and around myself to feeling more and more pain until I actually stepped out of our relationship for the first time when our daughter was three years old.

I couldn't stand the amount of pain that I was experiencing being around him anymore and decided to move near my parents. I got myself a fulltime job again and there was the pain of leaving the father of my daughter who I was still in love with but whose control I did not want to and could no longer bear.

For the first time in years I relived joy, freedom and independence in my life again and I felt whole, satisfied and liked myself again. That person I used to be, came to the surface again and it was as if I never changed which I knew, was not true of course. I lived in that pain-free state for about a year until a very defining moment occurred.

It saddens me to say that this game changer involved my mom, not to say that she was the reason for what was going to change my daughter's and my future but she was definitely a contributing factor. So, usually on every second weekend my husband would come to visit our daughter. He would come and pick her up to have her on the weekend and it happened that my mom had asked me to come over for coffee at the same time. That day I had to turn my mom down, explaining to her that George was going to arrive any moment to pick up Nathalie.

Then something unexpected happened. As it turned out, my mum envied me for choosing my husband over her. And so, suddenly, my living away from my husband was not this joyful experience anymore, either. It now filled me with pain, seeing that my mum was jealous of the father of my daughter. Should a grandmother not be happy that her granddaughter was able to spend time with her father? After all he has always been very caring and loving of her. Or, was it possible that my mum saw something that I could not see at the time?

Anyway, I started to rethink my options because my partner appeared to be very nice again and made promises of changing, pointed out that he could see his mistakes and apologized and reassured me that things would be different if we were together again.

Because of that incident I saw myself misunderstood by my mom which filled me with pain and on the other hand, I could see that moving back with my husband could absolutely be a good thing. It would surely be very much of an advantage for our daughter because I never wanted her to grow up without her father. She would be nurtured by both her parents at the same time again. And for me, it would be less stressful of not having to work full time, spending more time with our daughter and not having to support myself financially anymore.

I am sure, you get the picture. The tables had turned yet again. It pained me to live so close to my parents because I felt controlled by them, who were watching every single step of mine and my child's and it seemed very appealing to being back together with the father of my daughter to give her the opportunity of living with both her mum and dad under one roof again. What followed was us moving back to him again. I quit my 'quite prestigious' job of being the personal secretary of the owner of a well-known company in my home town and returned to live with my husband which I was so relieved of leaving only a year prior to that. Isn't life full of surprises at all times?

Not long after, we had our son and we decided to migrate to Australia.

As I shared with you earlier on, we had a vision that kept us focused on our goal, and things were working out quite well for as long as I spent all my precious time with my husband and the children, being there for them and the business all around the clock.

Once we had settled in and a sort of daily routine started to arise and with me starting to connect and make friends with other mums from school, family affairs came to a turning point yet again. As you know, when you have children, you get involved in social circles of moms from school as you share common challenges which could be either about teachers or your children themselves or even about yourself trying to juggle it all. You have got a lot of common grounds to chat about and in that way one can help each other out with difficult situations.

And it was exactly that occurrence, that led to a growing disliking in my husband and the more I ventured out, not doing anything wrong by all means, just usual motherly duties and fun stuff with other mums, the more controlling he became again.

So as far as I was concerned, the pain started to kick in again and after quite a few years of him being in charge and more disturbingly wanting to exercise his authority over me, I had reached a point where I knew I couldn't sustain that pain for the rest of my life and I became determined to change my situation.

CHAINS OFF - WINGS ON

It did not matter what and how much I did for my husband, he turned it around and said that I didn't act coming from my heart but purely out of selfish reasons. He managed to do that so persistently that the hurt that was caused by him acting like this seemed to burn a never healing scar into my heart and I felt my love for him dying little by little, sort of fading away bit by bit.

There was this one incident that comes to mind very vividly. Our son would have been around seven years old and I allowed him to stay at his friend's house in the afternoon. The following morning at breakfast he complained about some scratches on his leg from playing soccer with his best mate. As a result my husband just shook his head with a slimy grin on his face that such an injury would not have occurred, if I had not allowed David to go for a playday. But of course according to him, I was glad to have an afternoon off, where I did not have to look after our son. How sickening is that way of thinking that a mother allows her son to have a fun afternoon at his friend's house, but in the eyes of her husband she is doing it out of selfish reasons, not having to look after him.

You see, no matter what I did, in his mind it was never good enough and my actions came from being selfish and self-centered only.

So, I kept enduring the pain, thinking that staying in the relationship was the best for the children, so they were able to live with both their parents.

But how wrong was I! All the children did was witness the ugly and endless quarrels that were going on between their father and their mother. We created this harmful situation for them, rather than providing them with a caring and loving atmosphere.

In total, I endured the pain for another few years until it really became unbearable and I had to leave because I was at a point where I realized that if I stayed any longer, I would cease to exist. My core me would be burnt to pieces, shattered and buried under false accusations and I could not allow that to happen because I realized that it was very important not only for me but it was crucial for my children to stay sane and for me to keep my sanity.

LOVE IS NOT ENOUGH

As tough as it was, I decided to leave. Even though the love was still there, I had to leave because it didn't outweigh the control, the blame game and the recurring harming treatment that I got from my husband. At that time, it was purely pain that ruled my life and I knew that if I didn't leave, I would end up, taking medication to sustain and endure my everyday living.

And most importantly, I knew that leaving meant becoming myself again whereas staying meant giving myself up and the wonderful, adventurous, excited being that I used to be would entirely cease to exist, be wiped from the planet.

And that is the very reason which leads me to the conclusion that **love is just not enough in a relationship**. There are so many more factors that need to be considered to make a relationship sustainable, and that in fact, brings me to the model that I'd like to share with you, which is called

♣ APPROACH ♣

PAIN VERSUS PLEASURE.

As Anthony Robbins found out in his Dates with Destiny Seminars, we all do more to avoid pain than to achieve pleasure.

To give you an understanding of what Anthony Robbins means by that I would like to share the following graphics with you.

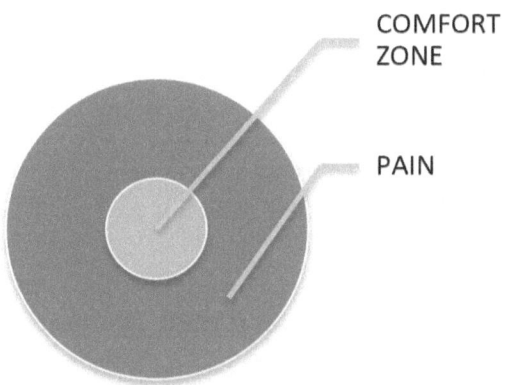

- Imagine being in your comfort zone, how snug, pleasant and homey it feels in there.
- Who wants to leave that cosy environment, right?
- Because pain is outside of your comfort zone, you keep trying to avoid it.
- So, the trick is, to reverse the model.

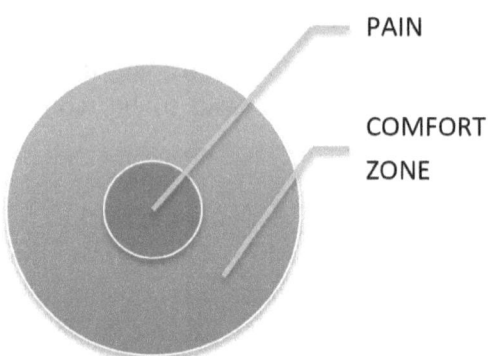

- Do you get the picture?
- What happens now when the pain is on the inside of your comfort zone and the pleasure on the inside?
- Wouldn't we all try to achieve the pleasurable state over and over again?

PAIN

According to Vicki Larson, a journalist and co-author of 'The New I Do, Reshaping Marriage for Sceptics, Realists and Rebels', "Six of every ten people are unhappily partnered and four out of ten have considered leaving their partner."

A study done by the National Opinion Research Center in the U.S. in 2014 revealed that the trend is getting worse, not better. People are getting less and less happy in their marriages as time goes on.

The Collins Dictionary describes Pain as 'the **Feeling of Unhappiness** that you have when something **Unpleasant** or **Upsetting** happens.'

We all have experienced emotional pain in our lives.

There is the pain:
- of letting go of a loved one because of death but even,
- letting go of a loved one to protect them because both partners have a different view on what the relationship should look like. One wants marriage with moving in with each other. The other one wants a loose, non-committing life with both living in their own homes.
  What I mean here is explained in a beautiful saying that a friend of mine told me:
  "Never keep the key to somebody else's happiness in your own pocket." - Unknown
- Staying in a hurting relationship for the children's sake.
- A typical example of enduring a destroying co-existence is staying because of fear of the unknown where you might ask yourself disempowering questions like:
  "How will I earn my living?"
  "Where will I live?"
  "Will I feel lonely?"
  "What will our friends think?"
  And the list goes on.

And then there is Pleasure which we find most of the time too hard to achieve, or we think it is out of our reach, because, remember: to access pleasure we need to step out of our comfort zone or change our thinking and imagine pleasure inside of our comfort zone rather than seeing it outside and impossible to tap into.

So, let me explain Pleasure first and then we get to the HOW to deal with both these emotions and also how to turn them around:

PLEASURE

"In France we have a saying,
'Joie de vivre', which actually doesn't
exist in the English language.
It means looking at your life as something
that is to be taken
with great pleasure and enjoy it."

by Mireille Guiliano

The Collings Dictionary explains pleasure as 'an activity, experience or aspect of something that you find very **enjoyable** or **satisfying**.'

How do you experience pleasure in your life? There are so many ways of perceiving pleasure, isn't it?

- It can be as simple as
    - watching your children play nicely and in peace with each other.
    - bake cookies with your children or
    - decorate the house for Christmas, for a birthday or whatever it is.

- In relationships it can be
    - going to the movies together,
    - enjoy a nice meal or even prepare the meal together for a change on the weekends,
    - plan a house together,
    - savour moments of common activities like running, going to the gym, etc. and the list goes on.

I am sure everybody comes up with a long list of emotions, activities and memories they connect pleasure with.

♠ ACTIONS ♠

PAIN VERSUS PLEASURE
How can we tap easily into the more rewarding and enjoyable emotion of Pleasure rather than allowing ourselves to linger endlessly in the emotion we so badly want to avoid, Pain? Let me show you in the following examples how we can reverse the drama into the magic of our lives:

Step 1:
As mentioned in the Approach Section of this chapter, the Inversion of the Model is the secret weapon - Imaging the pain inside your comfort zone and the pleasure outside.

For example:
Imagine you are a person who has been controlled in a relationship and therefore relate the fear of commitment with your next relationship.

So, to avoid the fear of commitment which is on the outside of your comfort zone, you prefer staying alone because that is where and how you feel safe and protected and good.

Now turn it around and think of another liaison as something safe and enjoyable, where you feel loved and comforted.

Let me put it into graph form to make it more visible for you to understand how effective the reversing will be:

You rather stay alone, because that is where you are feeling safe:

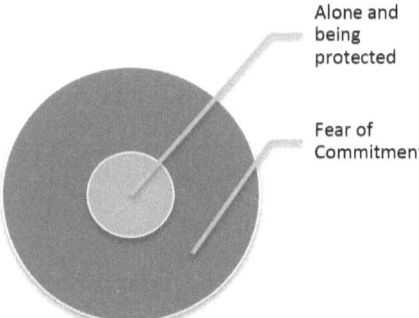

Now, change your thinking to being protected and being looked after in a relationship. All of a sudden, the fear of being alone is on the inside and the positive emotions of being protected in a relationship as your comfort zone is on the outside. So, that is what you are going for now. To stay within your comfort zone, you are breaking through the fear of being alone as demonstrated in the graph below:

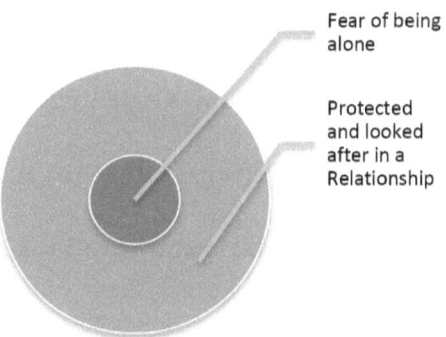

Step 2:
There is another approach to create enough leverage where 'the pain of staying the same' is enormously greater than 'the pain of changing'.

Usually, we are afraid of changing because we perceive more pain outside of our comfort zone, the unknown. So, by increasing the Fear within our comfort zone we are more likely to change.

In the above Model, imagine more painful emotions in your comfort zone, than only the fear of being alone. Maybe you could add:

- Fear of not being loved at all.
- Fear of missing out on many beautiful things a relationship can involve.
- Fear of never having children, if you stay that way.
- Fear of never having a family.
- Fear of whatever it is you love about being with somebody else. The choice is yours.

Can you see how that intensifies the fear within your comfort zone? And at the same time, you can add all the pleasurable emotions that come along with a happy affiliation. I am sure, by now you got the picture and know what I mean.

Step 3:
Another way to make change easier is, to have a big enough reason WHY. The reason WHY enforces our will power and therefore, we are more likely to succeed in our mission to change. It is a little bit similar to adding comforting and positive emotions to the outside of your comfort zone, but they must be linked to our will power. The more positive and strong reasons you can find to make the change, the easier it will be. Or yes, you have one single huge reason WHY.

Going back to the above example again, that reason might be:
- To prove somebody wrong
- Maybe you are sick and need somebody to look after you
- To break a family pattern
- ...

In general, what it comes down to for us to make a change is, to find out where we experience pain in our lives. Once we are clear about that we need to ask ourselves whether we are one hundred percent committed to make a change and whether we want it badly enough. And before we establish our plan of attack it is worth considering to accept help from outside because as a matter of fact, to try and do everything on our own is a lot harder. Sometimes it pays to swallow our pride and welcome support from others. We must be aware that if we have been stuck for a longer period of time, (in my case we are talking of a period of almost twenty years) we need to link an enormous amount of pain to the current situation to get ourselves in motion.

Remember: It needs a huge amount of effort to get a standing car rolling by pushing it. Once the car is in motion, the pushing gets easier until no more pushing is required at all. And we must not forget that it is our choice only. Blaming somebody else for the situation we are in, is not helping us move forward. We will self-sabotage our plans if we buy into the blame game.

So, take action now and start being responsible for your life. I could do it, so can you. I am not a super natural. I am just a woman like you who has made lot of mistakes but was never afraid of learning my lesson. Sometimes it took me falling over more than once as well before I started to listen to my inner voice and realized what was good for me.

So, don't be scared. What would be the worst that can happen?

♦ Abundance ♦
Spread your Wings

The best way to make this model your own and let it work miracles for you, is to complete the workbook activity below. Beware though that you must feel a huge amount of pain to be willing to make the change, otherwise all your trials will be in vain.

Look at the table down below and write down in the left column what causes you pain and in the left one what you are missing out on because of being stuck. I want you to really think about what it costs you being afraid of change.

ADVANTAGES OF STAYING IN YOUR COMFORT ZONE	WHAT ARE YOU MISSING OUT ON?

- Ask yourself, "What does staying the same give you that acting would not?"
- And also, "What do you like about that choice?"
- "What do you not have because of staying the same? What are you missing out? Keep piling on to the stack until it is obvious to you how you are sabotaging yourself.

- By asking yourself these questions and finding the answer to them, you leverage your pain, you add to it until it is too much to bear and you are willing to take the necessary steps to initiate the change.
- Now think about your reason WHY. It needs to be big enough for you to allow yourself to step out of your comfort zone.
- Then think about steps on how to move from the state of pain into the state of pleasure and on the actions that you need to take to make this transformation happen.
- What is involved? And what will the transformation give you? What will it allow you to do?
- Now, imagine yourself arriving at the finish line. You have done it.
- "What does it feel like?" "How do you feel?" "What can you see?" "Who is celebrating with you?"
- Allow yourself to stay in that moment long enough to experience what it would feel like if it was already your reality.
- I know it is not easy, it is a lot easier momentarily to stay in the state of pain than move away from it. But we talked about this before, it is only short term. In the long run, it pays off to go the extra mile to finally arrive in the zone of pleasure which is your

ULTIMATE GOAL.

Chapter Nine
We don't own them, We are Only here to Guide them

"The greatest gift you can give your children
are the roots of responsibility
and the wings of independence."

by Denis Waitley

♥ AWARENESS ♥

This chapter is about three Universal Fears, and in fact about us women becoming mothers. We all have to go through very similar circumstances from being young females not having any obligations, living for ourselves and enjoying life to the fullest without having to think about anybody else but being beautiful and shining to the moment when it all changes.

Our life the way it was before is turned upside down with the instant we fall pregnant.

Almost in a split second, our hormones start to go crazy turning us into either hysterical bitches of some sort, attacking our partners for telling us something insignificant like 'You look tired today darling' (of course we look tired, we are now nurturing and carrying around not only our own body but also the body of a little person growing inside of us), or crying sentimental creatures who are most sensitive to their environment and weep unstoppably just by looking at some cute babies in the animal kingdom.

And we are very much aware of the fact that our bodies will never look the same again for the rest of our lives and we are scared of how we would cope with the change and the very fact of giving birth. Midwives joke about, 'What goes in, also has to come out' – well in the moment of being in labor and enduring an ever so intense and crucial pain, none of us feels like joking or laughing about that – I think we all can agree on this one.

We are all given a nine-month period to get used to the idea of being a parent, a mother, and there is no real manual to cling on to. Of course, there are lots of books that you can read about what to do during pregnancy from eating healthy food to exercising. In fact, there is so much literature out there nowadays that I am sure for some young ladies it can be very daunting to find their way through the jungle of 'important' advices that 'must' be followed. And it does not stop there, the instructions continue and get more precise after the baby is born, on how to feed, when to feed them, what to feed them, etc., it's all there. The theory is given in books but in real life everything works out in a different way because every child is different and according to the circumstances they are born into, their needs vary as well. Who tells you what to do and how to take care of your baby when they are sick? Have you ever thought about that eventuality? Not all becoming mothers are in the lucky position of giving birth to a healthy capable child whose needs exceed the ones of a healthy baby by far. And us as parents, we are different as well, we cope with parenthood in certain unique ways, and the interaction between parents and children turns out to be very specific in each and every family as well.

As for myself – my parents and sister would remember me say it - I always said that I didn't want children because all that counted for me was my independence and success. I wanted to achieve something in life in my job. I had this picture of me being a successful business woman who earned her living and at the same time knew how to enjoy herself and have fun which never left room for having children.

What can I say, this conception of me being an independent successful working woman changed drastically with the moment I met my husband, because I fell deeply in love with him. I experienced a feeling that I had never encountered before, more than just being in love. There was this urge that started to rise from within me and as it turns out, the feeling was, that I would like to share something with him and so, suddenly I found myself thinking that maybe we could have a child together. – Oops, where did such an unfamiliar longing appear from all of a sudden. It seemed to come out of nowhere.

Can you believe this? Well, if you are a mother, then of course you know what I am talking about. So, my values and my life changed in an instant.

My partner and I started to talk about the possibility of having a child together and agreed upon trying. I stopped taking the pill and I thought that I would have plenty of time before falling pregnant and therefore did not really see the eventuality of falling pregnant ASAP.

But I was taught in a different way because, I think it was the second month that I wasn't on the pill anymore that I stopped getting my period. I also experienced low blood pressure which would result in my right ear going funny but because I was on a business trip in France and under a lot of pressure and stressed back then, I put the delay of the monthly bleeding and these symptoms simply towards these very convincing circumstances, and it would have never in my wildest dreams occurred to me that there was the possibility of me carrying a child.

Needless to say – I was wrong.

Oh dear, all of a sudden, I was hit with emotions that are very difficult to explain because on the one hand, yes, we decided to have a child and we were talking about it. We were planning on how it will be, will it be a daughter, will it be son, as you can imagine. But nothing was tangible because it was just a plan, just a discussion until that moment when I found out I was pregnant. At first, it hit me like a lightning bolt and I actually felt an enormous amount of fear arising in me. It was a fear that I had never felt before. I knew in that moment that my life would change forever. Nothing would be the same from now on.

Nothing would be the way it was before then. And I remember standing in front of the mirror and looking at my body. I was always very conscious of my figure and very happy with my looks. There I was standing in front of the mirror, looking at myself from all angles. And I was thinking to myself, "Remember this picture well because the way you look now, you will never look again." At the same time there was this feeling of sadness that was creeping up on me and I asked myself, "What did I do to myself? Why did I agree to go through that?"

Now, twenty-seven years later of course, I am very happy about having made that decision as I share a unique bond with my daughter and granddaughter and would not want to miss that for anything in my life. This feeling extends also to my son who is going to turn twenty-one this year and I am such a proud mother looking at how well my off springs turned out and what lovely and caring adults they have become.

Coming back to my story of finding out about my pregnancy, I must admit that it took me weeks before I could get excited about my new circumstances. It really took me a long time to adjust to the fact that I was going to be a mother and the word 'Mother' sounded so strange to me as well. I couldn't relate to it at all. Me being a mother, how weird was that. But anyway, I had a very nice pregnancy, I didn't have much morning sickness, everybody who saw me told me how beautiful I looked, how shiny and glowing I was, how my aura was blooming and everybody in my immediate environment agreed that the pregnancy suited me.

So, I was very happy and you all can relate to the moment when you start to feel the baby inside, how it moves around. It all starts with a little tiny tickle and then you can make out the actual movements until you experience the not-so-pleasant kicks into your stomach, the side or down below. These are the moments of happiness and excitement every mother can relate to, and we are so blessed to be able to experience that wonder of life growing inside of us that no man would ever be able to know the slightest what it feels like to us.

That is one of the few moments where I think that females have been advantaged by nature over males considering the multitude of issues we have to deal with - the monthly pain that comes along for some of us with the periods, the lifelong responsibility that we feel for our off springs, the way society still looks at us as being inferior to males and of course, the pain of giving natural birth plus the fact that we have to wear make-up and paint our finger and toe nails to look pretty and not to forget the ever so annoying 'hot flushes' when we go through menopause. Come on girls, do you agree that there are not many other occasions where nature has thought of us in a kind way in comparison to males?

Sorry, for being side tracked for a moment.

When I found out that I was having a baby and after having had time to accustom to the news, I got really excited and we both were very happy about the fact to become parents.

I was one of the lucky women who had a wonderful nine months which I absolutely enjoyed and birth itself, what can I say: It started with me feeling some unease in my tummy after being two days overdue and talking to my mum on the phone. When I informed her of this weird feeling down below occurring every 15 minutes, she advised me to go to the hospital right away as that would be the contractions already. What did I know? It did not even feel that bad.

So, I rang my partner and he took me into the delivery room. And would you believe it, two hours later, with no complications I was giving birth to my beautiful daughter, Nathalie. I was so happy to find out I was having a girl (I wanted the gender to be a surprise even though I always had a feeling that I was carrying a female) because I always wanted a daughter first. I don't know what my husband felt but for me, it was just a blessing.

The excitement and joy of becoming the mother of a little baby girl was dimmed immediately as I was told that something was not right with my daughter. As it turned out, she was born with an anomaly and was taken off me after only just initially feeling her laying, still wet and warm, rolled up in a tiny bundle, on my tummy after delivering her into our world. She was taken to a Pediatric Hospital away from me, because she needed instant surgery.

As you can imagine, I felt tested as a mother from day one onwards and for a whole year we were left in the unknown as to whether our little darling was going to be okay or not.

WE DON'T OWN THEM, WE ARE ONLY HERE TO GUIDE THEM

That is the year in which for the very first time in my life, I was confronted with one of the Universal Fears, the fear of not being enough.

I constantly feared of not being enough for my child, I repeatedly asked myself whether I was good enough as a mother. Was I giving my sick child everything she needed?

After having encountered the first one of the Universal Fears through my daughter, six and a half years later, I got taught another fear.

We had our son and when he was eight months old, we migrated to Australia which we planned on doing together as shared with you before and that is when both, my husband and I encountered the second of the Universal Fears, which was the fear of not belonging.

When we first arrived in Australia, we had no friends, no family, nobody to go to, we were just on our own to make this work, just the four of us, our two children, aged six and a half years and eight months, my husband and myself.

So, it was up to both of us to conquer the fear of not belonging. As for our children, the two of us had to be everything and everybody. We had to replace the grandparents, the uncles, the aunties, the cousins and in the beginning even the friends, because there was nobody in our immediate environment that we knew, not one familiar soul. And so it happened, that we both concentrated fully on our children, and we gave them as much love as we could to make up for the love that did exist for them on the other half of the planet. As a matter of fact, still to this day I believe that our children never had to experience the second of the universal fears of not being loved. Because even though there was no immediate family around with us here in Australia, my husband and I did everything to make our children feel loved and we were and still are always there for them.

I was always a strong believer that we must guide our children and let them make their own decisions to a certain degree. And I started practicing that with mine at a very young age. When they rebelled against some rule that we made we would say, "Yes okay, you can try it your way but just know that you might get hurt or whatever and don't come and say we didn't warn you." And that actually I did even when they were in their teenage years, the most critical years. I always pointed out to them that they have to live with the decision that they were about to make and so that's why I called this chapter, "We Don't Own Them, We Are Only Here To Guide Them".

From the moment they are ready to choose their own path, as hard as it is for us parents, we have to let them go and wish them all the best.

I know, there are some of you who would like to see their son or daughter go a certain path, thinking it would be the best for them. But, be honest with yourself, isn't it most of the times that you want your lost dreams to see lived through your children and not to save them from certain experiences? Or it could be your own fears governing the wish of your children taking on a certain path. Don't even try to do that because you disadvantage your children in the biggest possible way. By doing that you are blocking them off from their true destiny and they will find it immensely hard to get back to what was meant for them, if ever they are able to bounce back. I have witnessed it myself within my own family, an aunty who was driven for her son to become a doctor of some sort. He gave in initially and went to University but found himself unhappy and left his studies. He was kind of lost for a certain time and in the end, it took him almost half of his lifetime to find his true calling – how sad is that. And yet, I know that my aunty (her soul rest in peace) only meant the best for him.

Wouldn't you agree that it is unfair and doesn't make sense at all to oppress your longing onto your children and see them suffer at the same time?

As I said, we are all individuals with our own desires and fears, designing our own fate, driven by an inner craving that only each individual recognizes for themselves, no matter how young. Don't we all deserve to be free in the choice of designing our future to fit perfectly into that particular and unique human being, the blue print that the Universe has reserved for us?

For some of us it might be harder than for others, I know. We just have to keep reminding ourselves that it is never too late to live our dreams. It is a choice that we can make at any stage of our lives. It only depends on you if you are ready to fight those fears and rise as the person who you were meant to be from the beginning of your being.

As for your children, of course you will never stop guiding them and if you are good and caring parents, you will always invite them to come back when they are in need. They need the certainty that they can knock on your door any time and ask for your opinion, guidance and of course, support. In fact, I would go as far as to say that if they appear on your doorstep asking for assistance, it is a sign that you have done something right with their upbringing because obviously they value your opinion and they are certain that they can always rely on you. It means that they actually look up to you and they feel that they have been brought up in a caring, loving way and they still honor that now that they're adults.

As a matter of fact, we all love our children and want them to be happy, and we know we could save them from certain heartaches if they listened to us. But that is my point, we can only guide them. The final decision is up to them and that is the only way for them to push through their fears and to realize that it is not all that bad, and that by moving forward they are growing themselves and collecting their shaping, sometimes rewarding, sometimes devastating experiences. Every individual designs their own learning curve and we keep doing that until the day we are called to leave this plane.

So, guide them and support them in making their own mistakes when they need you most!

♣ APPROACH ♣

I am going to talk about THREE **UNIVERSAL FEARS** (In fact, there are more than only three Universal Fears, but I will be talking about the ones I consider to be the major ones):

NOT BEING ENOUGH - NOT BELONGING - NOT BEING LOVED

We all create beliefs unconsciously, which means we make them up outside of our awareness. These beliefs are designed for us to be enough, to belong and to be loved.

The quality of our up-bringing whether coming from parenting, teachers, mentors or anybody who influenced us along the way, determines the quality of our awareness level and therefore the quality of our beliefs.

Let me share with you the concept on how our identity is shaped:
- 0-2 **Egoless Phase:** Babies don't know any fears or danger. They are like a blank canvas, well cared for and looked after by their parents. They are in an egoless state and unconscious of what is going on in their lives

- 3 - 7 is the **Imprint Phase** of our lives. The Ego starts to kick in to protect our survival. By starting to interact with others, we develop certain beliefs about ourselves. Our environment begins to affect us. Different interpretations of our experiences make us into different people.

- 8 - 15 is the **Modelling Phase.** That is when the Three **Universal Fears** start to imprint the Code to our Belief System.

- 16 - 23 we call the phase of **Socialisation** which is when we start mixing socially with others and when we find a way that is acceptable to the society.

Everybody has these fears, that's why they are called Universal. Let's have a closer look on how these fears influence our lives.

♠ ACTIONS ♠

FEAR

"Fear doesn't exist anywhere
except in the mind."

by Dale Carnegie

According to the Cambridge Dictionary, the word "FEAR describes an **Unpleasant Emotion** of **Thought** that you have when you are frightened or worried by something dangerous, painful, or bad that is happening or might happen."

I also like the way Karl Albrecht PH.D. defines Fear: He says that fear is "an anxious feeling, caused by our anticipation of some imagined event or experience." According to him, Medical experts say that the anxious feeling we get when we're afraid is a standardized biological reaction. In other words, it is a feeling that just shows up. There is nothing we can do to prevent it.

What we can do instead is to choose, how to react to fear.

Fear is and always has been a vital response to physical threat and emotional danger. It is very unlikely that a child reaches adulthood with an intact self-esteem. Reason is, that they had to create certain behaviours and belief systems to survive. These belief systems are influenced by the Universal Fears.

So now, let's have a closer look at the three Universal Fears, how we create them, how they show up in our belief system and how we learn to live with them:

FEAR OF NOT BEING ENOUGH:

"The truth is: Belonging starts with self-acceptance.
Your level of belonging, in fact,
can never be greater than your level of self-acceptance,
because believing that you're enough is
what gives you the courage to be authentic,
vulnerable and imperfect."

by Brene Brown

According to the Cambridge Dictionary, "enough is **as much as is necessary**; in the amount or to the degree needed."

When it comes to us feeling enough, who actually determines whether we have reached the degree needed? Could it be that we determine that ourselves? - Absolutely and the reason why we do that is that over the years we have measured ourselves in comparison with others. Thus, we have created a belief that says, "We are not good enough."

Looking at the chart of how we and when we form our identity, we realize that this belief can be formed as early as us being two years old. All it comes down to, in creating beliefs around our fears, is the level of respect that is being given to us.

Let me give you some examples and how we as adults can approach some issues in a more careful, respectful way not to initiate the feeling of not being enough in our children:

DIS-RESPECTIVE WAY	RESPECTIVE WAY
I remember a time in my life when I wanted to learn how to play the flute. I was a beginner and might have had only one or two lessons and the teacher compared me with one of his students. There were two ways in which he could have handled the situation: "The girl who had her lesson with me before you, is doing a much greater job than you." That response gave me the feeling of not being enough and as a result I quit my lessons and never ended up learning how to play the flute.	"I know you are trying really hard and I respect that. I am sure if you keep practising you will be as good as that girl in no time." That has a much better feel to it, doesn't it? In that case, I would have been encouraged to continue to play the flute and would have even tried harder to get where I wanted to be.
Your child comes home with a bad report card and all you can say is, "Not again, what's wrong with you?"	In the very same situation you could say, "Oh dear, how do you feel about your results? What do you think went wrong?" And then you could offer your help in working out a plan of attack to achieving better grades in the next report card.

DIS-RESPECTIVE WAY	RESPECTIVE WAY
Your child is only a toddler and wants to help you with whatever it is you are doing, and you say something like, "No thank you sweety, you don't know how to do that."	Again, you could handle the situation in a much more positive and reassuring way for your child. Give them something little to do to be able to participate in your project, as insignificant the task might be, but it will build the muscle of self-esteem in your child and therefore make them feel enough.
Entering your child's room without knocking is very disrespectful.	It is much better to show your child respect by knocking on the door and asking if it is okay to come in.

Isn't it scary on how easily we can reinforce that fear of not being enough in our little ones? If we have been treated in a dis-respective way when we were little, we have already created the belief that we are not enough, and it will haunt us throughout our lives unless we learn how to deal with it and turn our belief patterns into ones that are more serving for us.

Now, let's look at the next fear which is the

FEAR OF NOT BELONGING:

"A deep sense of love and belonging is
an irreducible need of all people.
We are biologically, cognitively, physically
and spiritually wired to love, to be loved and to belong.
When those needs are not met,
we don't function as we were meant to.
We break. We fall apart. We numb. We ache.
We hurt others. we get sick."

Brene Brown (American author, born 1965)

The Cambridge Dictionary describes belonging as to **be in the right place** or a suitable place or to **feel happy** or **comfortable** in a situation.

The fear of not belonging is again created when we are between 8 and 15 years old, in the Modelling phase of our identity. Children can be cruel. It only needs one strong character in a group of peers who is to decide whom to let belong to their group and whom to spare out. That is the stage, when peer pressure can make us do silly things because we do want to belong to that tribe of peers.

As working adults, we know about that fear of not belonging when we get into an unfamiliar environment where we are the 'newbie' and don't feel like fitting in yet.

In a relationship, it might be the family of our partner we have trouble to fit in which is normal because we don't know that family's map of the world yet.

Sometimes it is even better not to belong for our own sake, yet it is difficult to see the benefits in that particular moment.

I am specifically thinking of a moment in my life where it hurt lots not to belong, yet I stayed strong because in a way I did not want to belong to that group of peers and at the same time I felt left out.

This particular incident happened when I was in high school back in Austria. The cellar where the central heating was located was allotted to pupils for smoking during recess. I can say that literally everybody from my class headed off into the cellar for smoking during every single break throughout the day. I tried smoking at that time once only and could not find any liking to it. Therefore, I spent most of the recess periods either by myself or with a few other 'uncool' people in the class room.

So, in that case 'not belonging' was an advantage but it cost a lot of courage, strength and belief in me not to be part of the majority. For a young person, whose self-esteem shows already cracks it would be maybe impossible 'not to belong' in that case.

And of course, there is our last of the Universal Fears, the

FEAR OF NOT BEING LOVED

"Being deeply loved by someone gives you strength,
while loving someone deeply gives you courage."

by Lao Tzu

The Cambridge Dictionary describes to love is 'to **like another adult** very much and be **romantically** and **sexually** attracted to them, or to have strong **feelings of liking** a **friend** or person in your **family**.'

The love we are talking about here is love without strings or rules attached, unconditional love, pure love. Everything else but pure love is considered a means to make somebody like or love you.

Let me give you some examples of pure love versus love as a condition:

PURE LOVE	LOVE AS A CONDITION
Parents love their children no matter what they do or have done.	Parents love their children only if they do what they tell them to do or if they become what they think is right for them or if they don't value and put into consideration their children's opinion, etc.
In a partnership, you love your partner in the way the marriage celebrant asks you to, "for good and for worse" and you try to work problems out when things get tough.	Love attached to a condition in a partnership might mean being loved only if you perform according to your partner's expectations or the rules your partner holds around you.
Self-love, the highest form of love in its pure form is of indispensable importance and value to a human being in achieving an outstanding enriched live. i.e. "I love myself the way I am because I know I have everything that I need within myself right now."	Self-love tied to rules that a person makes up for themselves to being loved is self-sabotage and does not serve a higher purpose. i.e. "I can love myself only if I lose x kilos or if I get my grey hair coloured or if I get that job, etc.

If we think we are not being loved for who we are, we cannot accept the circumstances and the very same will start to crush us.

In a relationship you might feel loved, but in reality you are only being loved as long as your partner has control over you (that was the case in my marriage) or if you do or don't do certain things, whatever it may be or as long as you fit into your partner's map of the world. Over time, you might outgrow that map and your partner does not accept the new arising YOU.

And the list goes on, I am sure by now you get what I mean with 'being loved'.

So, in conclusion to this chapter, remember this:

- The more we guide our children in a gentle, respecting way with a never-ending willingness to understand their point of view and where they are coming from, the more we help them create a life of abundance, joy and self- fulfillment with a healthy portion of self-esteem.

- Us, the parents from today, are the ones creating the future generation of tomorrow.

- Let them go when they are ready, don't hold them back from what they need to do to create their own life story.

- You have done anything and everything in your power to influence them to create their version of life in a righteous way.

- Don't expect them to do or want the same things as you do as we talked about in Chapter 8. We must respect their Map of the World to allow them to create their dreams.

- We don't own them, we can only guide them.

♦ Abundance ♦
Spread your Wings

The exercise for this chapter is a very simple, but very powerful one. As we are talking about Universal Fears which we all experience throughout our lives and which will pop up over and over again, I would like to take the liberty and remind you that the best remedy to counteract our fears, is to show gratitude.

So, all I am asking you to do in this chapter, is to start a GRATITUDE JOURNAL.

I want you to use this journal on a daily basis, whether you want to do the exercise first thing in the morning, after waking up or as your last thing in the evening before going to sleep.

Personally, I find that it is a nice way to start the day as you set yourself up for a wonderful day, filled with positivity and rewarding energy by showing gratitude as your first priority to a new day. But it is of course entirely up to you to choose what suits best for yourself.

Anyway, I want you to write down ten things which you are grateful for in your life. It can be the same things every day, or you come up with something new every time you open your journal. It does not matter. Start by writing down what comes into your mind immediately after reading this exercise and then continue doing it on a regular basis in your Gratitude Journal.

What matters is that you do this consistently over a period of at least two months.

After a certain time of showing gratitude on a regular basis, you will notice that certain matters will fall into place as if by magic.

As for your fears, you will notice that they lose their power over you.

Have fun and try to be as consistent as possible.

> ♥ It is in the regularity and repetition that we create
> the power for change. ♥

Chapter Ten
Enjoy the Ride

"Change your life today.
Don't gamble on the future,
act now, without delay."

by Simone de Beauvoir

♥ AWARENESS ♥

I thought it would be nice to end the book on a positive note and even though you and I and everyone else go through so much trouble in our lives, I want you to remember that there is an endless amount of beauty, abundance, excitement, adventure, and enlightenment around you.

Can I, therefore, please invite you to pause for a moment and really appreciate everything you are in the position to do, no matter how hard or delightful because as long as you breathe and are able to take in the beauty of our mother earth, you can consider yourself lucky. In the darker moments of life, just have a look around to those who are a lot worse off than you and extend your appreciation to the Universe in deepest gratitude.

Now, let me share the following story with you. You all know that life is a roller coaster, everybody has experienced it. In fact, it's a forever ongoing roller coaster with the most exhilarating ups that almost lift you into heaven and the worst devastating downs surrounding you with darkness and seeming helplessness at times. The moment you feel you are on the ride of your lifetime, something of the opposite nature happens and within split seconds, you see yourself plummet into the darkest corners of an endless ocean, filled with bewildering waves of fear, anxiety, hopelessness or whatever it may be!

I don't think there are ever some stable moments of longer duration, not that I personally have ever experienced endless occasions of just dancing on the tips of the waves, so to speak. I would say it only comes down to weeks or months of 'living the dream' until the tables turn around again. I don't know about you but sometimes it feels like falling into a deep hole as if slipping from the top of an icy mountain within no time at all. And to try and crawl back up on this mirror-like surface takes a huge deal of determination, effort, patience, and it certainly takes courage and a change in your thought pattern too.

So, the tale that I would like to share with you takes me back again to that disastrous year of repeating a class in High School, which then made it possible for me to finish High School with a breeze as this experience made me grow into a strong, confident person.

After finishing school in such a positive way, the question came up about what to do next? I asked myself, "What can I do now?" I didn't really have a plan. As a matter of fact, I knew what I wanted to do and that was to study Art History, but as it turned out, it was not meant to be.

I have always been artistic and enjoyed sketching, painting, drawing, craft you name it. And during my years of High School, I was able to immerse in the love of doing arts. I had a very good mentor and teacher in that respect, who actually wanted to see me take up painting as a career for my professional future. He wanted me to go further with it, as in studying Art and making a living from it. So, he was the one who suggested it to me to go to University and study Art History. Him recommending such a thing, wowed me, because I personally did not think that I was good enough to take on Art as a career path. But I loved his idea and as it was my biggest passion in those days, it made total sense to me.

But as mentioned before, it did not take long before the black clouds appeared on the horizon because studying Art History meant for me to go to Vienna, the capital of Austria which was about 200kms away from home. That again would result in getting an apartment in Vienna to move there and like all capitals, Vienna is a very expensive city and there was just no way my parents could have afforded that, even with me working while I was going to University. There were just not enough funds to do that. The financial difficulty and impossibility were black cloud number one.

The second dark opposing cloud was the way my parents, especially my dad thought about Art as a way of earning one's living. He always said that studying art undoubtedly is a breadless occupation. "You won't make it. It's nothing tangible, really if you want my advice, I would not do it if I were you." That turned my determination into insecurity and as a result, I then gave in. - Thinking back now, I dropped my dream far too easily. I did not try hard enough. I guess it was the easier option to let go of the idea and the question of what to do instead arose again.

I had no backup plan. When I was in primary school and early years of High School, I could always see myself as a teacher. But the idea of standing in a classroom full of children for the rest of my life – me, who never even wanted to have children on her own in first place – was not that colorful anymore and the idea of studying to become a teacher was dismissed there and then. In the end, I couldn't and didn't come up with a plan for what I wanted to do as an occupation for the rest of my life.

At that time, and for many more years to come, I had not the faintest idea what my life purpose would be.

From looking around, being curious what there was in options for me to do, I came across the possibility of going to France as a Nanny because I had been taught French for the last four years of schooling and I happened to really love the language – especially because of advancing to a grade A student after years of sucking in it. All I could think of was deepening my language skills by living in the country amongst French people, and at the same time it would be a way for me to venture out into the world and detach myself a little from the cosy little tucked away village St. Ulrich which I called home. - The fact that

CHAINS OFF - WINGS ON

I had to deal with children did not frighten me and I would find out later that Antoine, the little six months old baby I would look after, was very cute and I grew very fond of him in the end.

Originally, my parents agreed with me becoming a French Nanny because the plan was, for me to stay in Paris only for two months over the summer holidays. That was a thought, my parents could live with. They knew that after two months they would have their first born come back home again.

And so, it happened one day that I saw myself on a train to Paris. Let me assure you that this event was quite a defining moment in my life. As I shared with you earlier on, I was this protected girl from a village with 2500 inhabitants, a village where everybody knew each other, talked to each other and where every little corner looked familiar to me. Now, all of a sudden, I found myself in the sleeping compartment of a train, on a twelve-hour ride with no familiar faces to look at, travelling into the nowhere, the unfamiliar, the unknown. I had no idea what the family would be like, whose nanny I was going to be. All my parents and I did, was rely on the agency who helped us pick a family, not really knowing what these people would be like. What if the profile they gave to the agency was not truthful? – Quite a scary thought if you are away from your loved ones for the first time all by yourself, don't you think?

Well, as for me, I dismissed negative images like that as soon as they came up in me while I was travelling, as I was determined to make this the best time of my life. After all I just had finished school and I had no plans for the future. I was young and free and was filled to the brim with an endless amount of certainty that I could take on the whole world and my entire being was overflowing with an ever-so-huge amount of curiosity about what my future would hold for me.

As you can imagine, everything planned out very well. The French family welcomed me into their lives and treated me very well. They expected me to earn my living with contributing to the cleaning, cooking and child-minding chores but accepted and treated me like one of theirs. I spent the two months of holidays with them in La Trinite, La Bretagne, the Ouest of France at the Atlantic Ocean, which was the most beautiful I could have asked for. I loved it.

Looking back, I think, it was there and then when my passion for the sea sparked. I always adored the weeks during summer holidays when my family took us to the sea in either Italy or the former Yugoslavia, where I would collect sea shells with my sister along the not-so-sandy but sometimes gravel-like beaches and inhale the salty breeze emanating from the waves which would cool me down on a hot day jumping, rolling and swimming in them. But spending two months in a row living by the sea, and I mean living, because it took only a one or two minute walk from the beach house to the actual beach, was a whole new experience which will stay with me for the rest of my life. In the end, I was so thankful for being able to stay with the Dorges family at their summer residence that I was sad having to leave them at the end of the holiday season.

I was supposed to return home after the two months, wasn't I?

But, here it comes: I was not ready to do that. I just started to like my independence (I wonder if that is where my strong desire for independence origins from) and the sense of adventure of living in a foreign country. And I was filled with pride about the huge progress I had made in deepening my French language skills. So, I decided to stay in Paris. Of course, that meant that I had to shift to another family as my original family did only want a baby sitter for the holiday period. This new family was one with three boys who were full on, they were nine months, three years and five years old and they lived on the outskirts of Paris, the sons of two doctors.

To me, where they lived, wasn't even Paris anymore because it took me an hour on the RER, that is the fast train to go into the city (a bit like the metro but for the suburbs further out) and I must admit that travelling on it at night time was not something I would ever recommend to a young girl by herself (if you get the picture). In total, I was supposed to stay with them for the rest of the year.

Yes, correct, I was supposed to stay there for a whole year but already after spending one month with them, I knew that I could not and did not want to stay with them for that long. I felt home sick because they treated me like a nanny only, I was not really one of them. I lived in the granny flat at the end of the garden and did not even have hot water. To have a hot shower, I had to walk over into the family residence which was okay while the temperatures were still around 20 degrees but with autumn and winter coming, I can assure you that I dreaded getting out of bed every single morning, knowing that I had to do the ice walk over to the main building and back.

As for the three little boys, they were full on and there were lots of situations in which I did not know how to handle them correctly, after all I had no education on how children's psychology works, on how to trick children and get them to do what they did not want to do. On many occasions I remember, not being in charge of the situation, it was rather them taking charge over me – if you see what I mean.

Luckily, I always stayed in touch with the Dorges family and at last after finding out how unhappy I had become, they offered me to stay with them as their nanny for the rest of the year.

Now, the tables had changed for the better again for me and I was thrilled to be able to stay with my family in the center of Paris, the sixteenth 'arrondissement'. That alone made an immense difference to my happiness and wellbeing because it meant that I could join in the fun and go out with friends at night time. My days were cut into two halves, one of which I would be working as a nanny and the other one I would be going to La Sorbonne, the Parisienne University to learn French grammar, and also the Chamber of Commerce to learn the Commercial way of French.

And there it was, that defining moment for me, in which I blossomed from the country pumpkin into the city rose!

From one second to the other, I was in a world-known city in the middle of so many different cultures, people from so many different backgrounds and so many of them I was lucky to call 'my friends'. And the one language that combined us all was French, our second language, as good or as bad as it was, but we all were united by speaking French. What an awesome realization!

To say, I loved it, would be an understatement. I was like the butterfly that had been trapped in its cocoon for so long and then shed his outer protective layers, purely to evolve into this colorful amazing being, able to spread his multi-colored painted wings, allowing him to glide on the soft cushions of air right above everything else to discover the endless possibilities of his existence. And so, it happened to me. I was no longer that well-protected, innocent girl from the tiny unknown village in Austria who never had contact with what was going on in the outer world. I had become a cosmopolitan young lady who was in touch with many different corners of our beautiful whole wide world and touched by the people who called themselves 'my friends'. I had become a city girl.

As one can imagine, when that year came to an end and it was time for me to finally return back to Austria to my disliking, on the one hand, because of leaving so many friends and worldly memories behind. Memories also created from visiting the big well-known art galleries where all the original paintings of famous painters were displayed, the ones impressing me most, being the masters of the Impressionism. On the other hand, to my joy because of being reunited with my real family again, my mum, dad and my sister. I knew that I had kind of outgrown life at the village where my parents lived and I decided at that time that one day, I would be going to branch out again to live elsewhere.

But when I first came back, I made use of the French that I was able to deepen to a point where one would not even pick me for a foreigner amongst a French-speaking crowd and I started to tutor students who were about to finish High School. I can pat myself on the shoulder and say that I was very successful as a tutor.

The reason for my achievements in teaching French was a system that I had in place that worked with everybody whom I tutored. It was a step by step system that I had developed along the way which helped me personally get the grasp of this very challenging language with all its genders, declinations, etc. you name it. I knew it worked for me and therefore, I had the certainty within me in passing it on to my students. It was a very structured way for them to slowly get the hang of that difficult language in a logical way where I made sure, the studied topic was imprinted into their brains before moving them to the next topic.

And that is exactly what I have tried to establish by writing this book. I want you to accept this message as a step by step guide in assisting you to find your true self and with it, what is important to YOU only. Realize that you need to be selfish to a certain point and gift your soul what it needs and deserves to find true happiness and contentment. To achieve a state of full enlightenment, sometimes it takes drastic change, other times just minor ones.

Don't be afraid of what is going to happen by stepping out of your comfort zone. If you are unhappy now, it can only get better but the first step must come from YOU.

YOU must be willing to help yourself and only then, the Universe offers its support and guides you along the way.

And to help you to get on your way initially, to kick off the change with the first step, the turning point that you have been dreaming of for so long and that you deserve but have been dreading to take, I am explaining to you the models.

They will enable you to work through your challenges step by step and by making them your own and working through your problems, in the end you will succeed by resolving the problems by simply sticking to that structure.

That is my aim with this book.

Looking back at my life, I can say that I'm proud of what I have achieved and how far I have come. Now is only the beginning of something new and great that will be the base and the passion and the purpose for the rest of my life.

Please have faith and trust in me when I share with you at this moment that I cannot impose enough on the truth which is, to enjoy the ride of your life to the fullest!

The fact that you are born into the being you are, is a gift and it is up to you to accept this present for what it is and help it bloom into a marvelous, never to be forgotten experience. It is your story, so make sure it is a great one to tell.

No matter which way it is going, just remind yourself that it is YOU determining the direction in which your ride is going and that it is YOU who determines the outcome of the very same as well.

Learn how to dream. Have a positive, big outcome in mind and that is what you're going to get. Trust me, it is well worth it and even better if you put your thoughts and dreams down onto paper.

On this occasion, please allow me to share another model with you which will be the last one that I'm going to introduce you to. You already have a nice variety of structures that are there just waiting for you to have a play with and make them your own to overcome your life's challenges and rise up and above and beyond your fears and evolve into the magnificent human being that you always were meant to be.

This particular model you can actually make your own in every single circumstance of your life and you will grow through it from the start to the end, over and over again because that is what life is all about. Life is a continuous chain of never-ending change and because of the never-ending change, we never stop growing. We evolve until the day we cease to exist.

So, please pay attention to how it works and apply it and have a play with it as soon as you can.

♣ APPROACH ♣

TRUST ME MODEL
This model is a model that never ends because it is an exploration of the level of thinking we are at. It is a cycle for the challenges we are

facing. There are seven levels to this model and from level one to seven we are challenged to evolve in our level of thinking.

As soon as we hit the seventh level, we are confronted with starting from ground zero again.

The seven levels are:

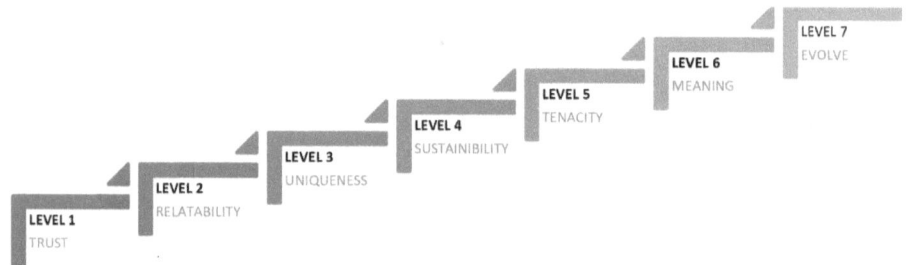

TRUST:
A person at this level of thinking does not trust anybody. They are very fearful and only focused on their survival. You could relate a person at this stage to a cave man swinging his cane at anything there is around. Everything in his proximity means danger. That person has not found their identity yet. They don't share any values with others and might not even have connected with their own values yet. To a person with that kind of thinking, a simple unknown phone call can be assumed as threat, or even issues with the bank, the tax department or other official departments.

RELATABILITY:
A person with this level of thinking can only relate to people who have proved themselves to them. They share similar values but they still have not quite found their identity and are too afraid to step away from the tribe. In the case of the cave man, they will only connect if the other person puts their baton down. A change happens if they are sick and tired of the same patterns and want to step out of their tribe. That is where and when they find their ...

UNIQUENESS:
That is the phase where the identity of the person starts taking shape. They realize that they don't have to live the way the tribe says they have to. At the same time though they are still too afraid to leave their

support group, yet they start being selfish. The ME starts kicking in, they are ME focused now.

Does reading that ring a bell to you? Yes, exactly we talked about a similar state earlier on in Chapter 6 where we went through the phases of the Adult Growth Model where the Rebellion refers to this stage of thinking. Once someone's identity has shaped enough, that person is ready to step their thinking up to ...

SUSTAINABILITY:
Now the person has found their uniqueness and they are ready to step out of the tribe. They realize that they have to overcome setbacks to form their character and are therefore proactively seeking challenges. (That was me in the beginning of the relationship with my husband when I thought no matter how many obstacles there come, I will be able to overcome them all because I love him so much). But that level of thinking does actually not do you any favours, you just make the everyday living harder for yourself, yet it does not give you any results which brings us to the next level of ...

TENACITY:
Now that person is aware and 'smart' enough to only seek out challenges that build their character and provide them with the desired results. They are prepared to step out of their comfort zone to build wealth and success. They are in search of obstacles to find out more about themselves and then they pause for a moment and ask themselves if that was all there is which moves them to ...

MEANING:
All of a sudden, all that they have achieved seems not enough and they ask for the meaning behind it. They are running out of challenges and feel like they have hit the roof, the pinnacle of their success. And in questioning themselves about how to continue, they realize that they have to ...

EVOLVE:
They now have realized that beyond the roof there is an abundance of more daring and life-changing opportunities they have never explored

before in their lives. And as if by magic new and the most amazing things will happen. That is the point where we start a new adventure or venture again in which we evolve through the different stages of the TRUST ME MODEL yet again.

Like I said in the beginning of this chapter, life is a never-ending spiral and we never stop learning. Now let me give you examples of the different levels of this model and how you can use it to your advantage when it comes to your relationship:

♠ ACTIONS ♠

TRUST

"You can't connect the dots looking forward;
you can only connect them looking backwards.
So you have to trust that the dots will somehow
connect in your future.
You have to trust in something -
your gut, destiny, life, karma, whatever.
This approach has never let me down,
and it has made all the difference in my life."

by Steve Jobs

The Collins Dictionary describes trust as 'a **belief** that **someone is good and honest** and will **not harm you,** or that something is safe and reliable'.

As mentioned earlier on, a person at this level of thinking is fearful of everything. They might be afraid to answer the phone because it could mean bad news. They might be even scared of opening the door to strangers out of fear of the unknown.

Let me give you some examples of people at that level and what it looks like for someone who has moved past this level of thinking.

PERSON WITH LACK OF TRUST	PERSON WITH TRUST
My ex-husband would not answer any phone calls with private number. And during our divorce he rejected any kind of paperwork from my lawyer and when my lawyer was forced to serve him with papers, he even insulted the person delivering the documents. He was held back by fear which is a result of lack of trust.	Had he moved past that stage, a simple phone call would not represent a threat to him and during the divorce he could have been more cooperative.
A person who is controlling and needs to know all the time where his/her partner and the children are falls into this category.	That same person would be okay not knowing where his partner and the kids are because he trusts his partner to take good care of them.
People who have no friends because somebody could hurt them are lacking trust.	People who are able to make friends and are able to maintain friendships have the necessary amount of trust.

Some people never move out of that stage of thinking and it really hurts to watch but it is up to them to say enough is enough. "I am done living that way and want to make an effort to move on to the next level which is …"

RELATABILITY

"Try not to get lost in comparing yourself to others.
Discover your gifts and let them shine."

by Jennie Finch

The Cambridge Dictionary describes Relatability as 'a **quality** that someone can **understand or feel sympathy for.**'

Like mentioned earlier on, a person at this level of thinking has not found their identity. They start to open up to others but still don't take ownership of what happens in their life. They only feel safe in a group of people who are like them. Some example down below again:

PERSON IN RELATABILITY	PERSON WHO HAS MOVED ON
A group of likeminded people go out for a drink and have a conversation going on between themselves. As soon as an 'outsider' tries to take part in their conversation, the energy of the group changes and they start joking because that new person represents a threat to them.	That same group of people having outgrown the level of relatability would have friendly welcomed the 'outsider' as an equal and included him in their conversation.
You are unhappy in your relationship and bitch about your partner to your friends.	You are unhappy in your relationship and take ownership of what is going on, you know what needs to be done to make the necessary adjustments.
Even though your partner's friends annoy you, you still come along with him/her by justifying to yourself that you have to do that for the sake of your relationship.	You have moved passed the stage of relatability and you own up to your partner and tell him to see his friends without you because you prefer to hang out with your own group of friends or prefer staying home.

A person with this level of thinking has got friends who are at their level and once they move on, they realize that they actually have outgrown that group of peers and they get bored or feel stuck and are ready to move on to the next level which is ...

UNIQUENESS

"Never stop fighting until you arrive
at your destined place - that is, the unique you.
Have an aim in life, continuously acquire knowledge,
work hard, and have perseverance
to realize the great life."

by A. P. J. Abdul Kalam

The Oxford Dictionary describes Uniqueness as 'the **Quality** of being **the only one of its kind** or of being particularly **remarkable, special or unusual**'.

Finally, the person has found their identity, connected with it and said to themselves, "Enough is Enough." They are no longer a follower. They have found themselves and know what is best for them. At the same time though, the tribe you just stepped out from represents a threat and you are rebelling against them.

DYSFUNCTIONAL UNIQUENESS	FUNCITONAL UNIQUENESS
You are too focused on the differences of opinion. So you decide to step out of the relationship, because you think that you are both too different.	You notice that there are a lot of differences between you and your partner. And you have a conversation about allowing each other your own space or your uniqueness, while still maintaining a healthy, loving relationship.
You are sick and tired of being in an unhealthy and unhappy relationship and decide to step out of it and start a new life all by yourself.	You step out of the unhappy relationship and realize that with the help of others, it is a lot easier and therefore accept their help.
You realize that you have outgrown the group of friends you have always been hanging out with. Your values have changed and you start judging them for their ignorance, and you decide to move on.	You know you have outgrown that group of friends but in many ways they are still very valuable for you. Know what your values are and be okay to express them if need be, but at the same time you don't have to declare them all the time or impose them on others. You can still be a part of that group of people, and when a discussion arises where you don't agree with them, you just observe the conversation instead of trying to prove or defend your point. e.g. - turned vegan - stopped bitching/complaining - stopped drinking too much alcohol - stopped eating sugar

DYSFUNCTIONAL UNIQUENESS	FUNCITONAL UNIQUENESS
	coins always make **sounds...** but **paper moneys** are always **silent.** so, when your value increases, keep **yourself silent** and **humble.**
A child at school who found his uniqueness and rebels against everybody and everything. (In this example, of course the child's carers and teachers have a huge responsibility in making the most of his uniqueness so it doesn't turn out to be a dysfunctional expression)	The child has found his uniqueness and knows how to use it to his advantage, thanks to the guidance from his parents, teachers and any other carers involved.

Finding one's uniqueness is a beautiful moment in life. It is a state that we cannot maintain forever unless we move to …

SUSTAINABILITY

"Resilience is all about being able to overcome the unexpected.
Sustainability is about survival.
The goal of resilience is to thrive."

by Jamais Cascio

The Cambridge Dictionary describes **Sustainability** as 'the quality of **being able to continue over a period of time'**.

The person realizes now that leaving the tribe and building one's uniqueness causes them to fail and they experience setbacks. They learn how to deal with the setbacks and build sustainability around them by avoiding them all together:

Examples:

Living by somebody else's values is not sustainable over time. The moment you realize that, you will make the necessary changes.

DYSFUNCTIONAL SUSTAINIBILITY	FUNCTIONAL SUSTAINIBILITY
Saving money to a point where your family is not cared for with their vital core needs (i.e. starving) is unsustainable.	Saving money to move forward in life is healthy.
Stifling restrictions in a relationship to the point where one is not allowed to do anything without the other is not sustainable.	Healthy boundaries for both partners are sustainable though.
One partner imposing on the other and dictating them what to do and how to do things.	Both partners agree on what needs to be done but give each other the freedom on how to carry it out.
Putting on a face and hiding your true self just to impress somebody is not sustainable because sooner or later your true self will surface whether you are planning to or not.	Being yourself, even if it seems you don't impress the other person, will definitely get you further in the long run than hiding who you truly are.
Making out of sharing the same interest does not work long term, i.e. making the other person believe that you like football which in reality you hate.	It is best to put the cards on the table straight away. At least each of you knows who you are dealing with.

Once you have mastered the level of Sustainability, you then move on to …

TENACITY

"A wedding anniversary is the celebration of
love, trust, partnership, tolerance and tenacity.
The order varies for any given year."

by Paul Sweeney

The Cambridge Dictionary describes **Tenacity** as the '**determination to continue** what you are doing'.

Determination is the key to building one's character. At this level of thinking, a person is ready to conquer all challenges. The more challenges, the more one deepens his identity.

DYSFUNCTIONAL TENACITY	FUNCTIONAL TENACITY
Being determined to pursue a goal for somebody else and in the end suffering yourself is dysfunctional.	Pursuing your goal because you are convinced that it serves your purpose and is doable is functional.
Challenging your partner just to find out his/her limits.	Challenging your partner for your partner's sake because you can see the potential.
Being determined in an obsessed way and therefore losing sight on what your objectives were originally.	Being determined and keep going until crossing the finish line.

And then comes a point when after hitting and successfully dealing with obstacles, we ask ourselves: "Is that it or is there more to it?" And we question the …

MEANING

"To live is to suffer,
to survive is to find some meaning in the suffering."

by Friedrich Nietzsche

The Cambridge Dictionary says that 'the meaning of something is **what it expresses or represents**'.

At this level of thinking, a person has achieved it all - Or did they really? Is that it? Well, that is the question. You think you have reached the pinnacle of your success - yet, hang on a moment - there might be more.

DYSFUNCTIONAL MEANING	FUNCTIONAL MEANING
You have been in a harmonious wonderful relationship. Your children are all grown up and now you feel kind of lost because your purpose, the purpose of bringing up and looking after the children has vanished.	You have been in an outstanding relationship and brought up children who are grown up and have left the nest and you start looking for another challenge in your life to have a new perspective and meaning again.
Your partner has been nagging you to stop smoking for health reasons but you ignore their warning and keep smoking anyway.	You partner wants you to stop smoking and because you are aware of what it could mean to keep smoking, you quit.
You have won over a life-threatening disease and are kind of lost because nothing means anything to you anymore.	You have battled a disease successfully and are keen to start from ground zero again to give your life new meaning.

After having dealt with the meaning of life in a functional way, you are then forced to progress to the next level which is …

EVOLVE

"Life is a moving, breathing thing.
We have to be willing to constantly evolve.
Perfection is constant transformation."

by Nia Peeples

According to the Cambridge Dictionary, evolve means 'to **develop gradually,** or to cause **something or someone to develop gradually**'.

Here we are - Whereas a person at the MEANING level of thinking perceives having hit the ceiling in his progress, the person at the EVOLVE level of thinking looks beyond that apparent glass ceiling, only to realize that there is a whole new dimension of challenges awaiting them. They discover a new set of challenges that they never experienced before. And thus, life is a constant stream of change. All you need to do, is being flexible to respond to any kind of change accordingly. Look at change as something exciting, exhilarating, and adventurous bringing along with it a whole set of new learnings, experiences, friendships, knowledge, etc.

In the state of EVOLVE, you will never be bored because you will catch yourself constantly looking for something unexplored, not yet conquered, something that will stretch your imagination and enlarge your capability of expanding your vision to evolve into the unimaginable. And you will be exhilarated and proud of yourself and never have regrets when the day comes when you have to leave this dimension to move on. – How wonderful is it, to be able to say good bye knowing that you have done it all, that you have lived to your full extent and your fullest potential!

Isn't that what we all should strive for, to not have any regrets?

Remember this:
– We never stop learning.
– Compare that saying with the Trust Me Model – doesn't that prove the wisdom of the above saying?
– Live is a never-ending learning curve.
– Always recall Anthony Robbins' words "The Ultimate Lack of Movement is Death".

All I would like to give you on the way from this chapter is to:

ENJOY THE RIDE OF YOUR LIFE

♦ Abundance ♦
Spread your Wings

As always at this section of a chapter, I find it most powerful to achieving results to find a peaceful moment and also some special place where you can focus on the exercise in an uninterrupted way. So, please consider these recommendations before moving further.

When you are ready to come along on a journey to your inner core, please find the answer to the following question and go from there:

What is bothering you the most at the moment in or about your relationship?

Think about the situation that you would like to change and imagine vividly how you would like it to be. Once you have found the answer to that task, I want you to see what it would look like, to feel what it would be like and what you would be telling yourself in that desired state of being.

Remember that place where you have gone to now and then I invite you to experience a breathing exercise which will only take a few minutes once you know what to do. And this particular exercise you can repeat whenever you feel it is necessary for you to recharge your batteries with the positive empowering imagination of your desired outcome. The method is from Richard Bandler, one of the creators of NLP (Neuro Linguistic Programming) and I heard it for the first time during my studies, used in a life coaching demonstration from one of our professional coaches. It is a very powerful but simple gift that I would love to share with you my sister.

Let's get started:

- If you are wearing shoes, I would like you to take them off and be barefooted. Sit upright on a chair with your hands in your lap in a kind of open position.

- Let your shoulders relax.

- Take a deep breath in through the soles of your feet (I know, that's not how it really works but I want you to feel as if you were breathing in through your feet).

- Feel the breath enter your body through your soles going into your calves and feel it rising up through your knees, thighs, hips, right into your tummy and up through your chest into your shoulders.

- Then breathe out and with breathing out, release all the tension and feel how it is leaving your shoulders.

- Then take a deep breath again and feel it rise through your body again, through your calves, knees, thighs, hips, tummy, chest, and into your shoulders.

- Now release even more tension from your shoulders with your out-breath.

- Breathe in through your soles one last time and try and hold your breath a little bit longer in your tummy before letting it rise up into your chest and into your shoulders.

- Now, release all the tension there is until you find yourself in that beautiful place that you have found earlier on and where you want to end up being.

- Stay there a moment and trust that you are exactly where you are meant to be.

- Let all the noise float by and notice your normal breathing.

- If there is still something that is bothering you, let go off it through your shoulders. Maybe you want to move your neck or shoulders to make the tension slip out and leave your body, whatever it takes for you to see it go.

ENJOY THE RIDE

- Now, travel to your third eye region between your eyes and pretend looking into your third eye.
- Notice how light and freeing it is in this moment. Stay there and soak up the lightness as much as you can.
- Focus on this moment.
- And now I want you to notice that you can choose to do anything right now.
- Feel all the positive strengths that you want for yourself (whether it be confidence, courage, excitement...) and know and trust that all these positive attributes and abilities where in you all the time.
- Now, take your right hand and put it onto your heart.
- In your mind's eye, float down into your heart and float around and notice what you see.
- Hold onto that feeling and notice what you are telling yourself.
- When you leave that space and come back into the now, I want you to write down all the details that you have seen or felt or heard, as detailed as possible.

Know that you can travel to that special place anytime you want and when you need to. It does not take more than five minutes, you can even escape into a bathroom and travel to your special place to recharge yourself with whatever it is you need there and then.

How easy, but effective.
All there is to say for me now, is:

♥ **ENJOY THE RIDE** ♥

Chapter Eleven
Forgiveness – your Most Precious Jewel

"The weak can never forgive.
Forgiveness is the attribute of the strong."

by Mahatma Gandhi

♥ AWARENESS ♥

Only after eleven years of being bitter, frustrated and disillusioned about my failed marriage, I am now harvesting the fruits of forgiveness towards my ex-husband but most importantly, towards myself. I never understood why he was still so angry with me for leaving him after so many years.

Now, I have the epiphany that it all had to do with my attitude, my view on our relationship and my view on the world in general, and the fact that all that time I had not forgiven him for how our marriage pended out. What I mean by that is, that I still could not forgive him for verbally abusing, controlling and threatening me and disrespecting our daughter for the beautiful young woman she was growing into. I have never been told the secret that lies behind all the negativity that you seem to attract which solely comes from your own thought patterns. The importance lies in HOW you think and not WHAT you think. Thoughts are happening anyway, you cannot stop them, but you can language meaning to them and rather be the observer of your thoughts than living them. Because as soon as you give Meaning to your Thoughts, you create Feelings.

Well, as I said before, my thought pattern had to change and I was made aware of that by my sister. As I was saying my good-byes to my family after one of the many beautiful emotional visits back home to Austria, my sister Birgit surprised me with a good-bye present before leaving to the airport. Her gift to me was a tiny little paperback book (weight always plays a big role when you are travelling on a plane) about a Hawaiian forgiveness ritual called Ho'oponopono, written by Ulrich Emil Dupree, originating in the findings of Dr. Ihaleakala Hew Len.

This is actually believed to be one of the most powerful, if not the most powerful rituals for forgiveness.

♣ APPROACH ♣

HO'OPONOPONO
Ho'oponopono is a spiritual cleansing ritual which is used to liberate yourself from anxiety, negative thought patterns and blocks that hinder you from moving forward and growing.

You and me, we are all supposed to have a fulfilled and happy life but by hanging on to anxiety, frustration, confusion, emptiness, and whatever your negativity and destroying feelings might be, you exercise self-sabotage at its highest level. You stand in your own way on the road to happiness. To let positivity and happiness into your life that most of you crave for, you must be prepared to let go of any unresourceful patterns.

And Ho'oponopono is the perfect tool to master that process of letting go and liberating yourself. It is a very simple process and consists of only four simple sentences which are:

"I am sorry."
"Please forgive me."
"I love you."
"Thank you."

Let me explain in the following, how it is done:

♠ ACTIONS ♠
Forgiving is to receive healing in return:

CHAINS OFF - WINGS ON

"Healing is a matter of time,
but it is sometimes also
a matter of opportunity."

by Socrates

The Cambridge Dictionary describes the word forgiving as 'to stop blaming or being angry with someone for something that person has done, or not punish them for something'.

That description says it all: "Stop blaming somebody else for what is happening or not happening to you." Therefore, it is of utmost necessity to start the forgiveness process with yourself. Only once you have healed yourself, you can then move on to healing the relationships you have with others.

I am giving you this wisdom in my last chapter, just in case you still have not found what you were looking for in all of the coaching models and exercises from the previous chapters. The reason for not feeling the fulfilment that you are seeking, might be YOU.

It looks to me as if you have to start healing yourself right now by forgiving yourself. And I mean right now, not any time in the future, but right now in this moment.

I invite you to stay with me and read carefully what the four sentences mean individually:

1. "I am sorry".
   By saying that, you actually accept all the impureness in and about yourself. You accept that you have contributed to either your own or other's suffering and you express that you truly are sorry about that.

2. "Please forgive me."
   With these words, you ask for forgiveness for causing pain to yourself and others. I am mainly talking about mental suffering by not accepting somebody the way they are or judging them or bullying them or whatever it might be because these actions have

violated the universal harmony. By asking them for forgiveness, you get them to liberate you, to let you off the hook.

More important than forgiving others, is the fact of forgiving yourself for not loving yourself, for not accepting yourself, for doubting yourself, etc.

3. "I love you".
   By saying you love them and you love yourself, you admit that you accept them and yourself with all the flaws and impurities and you acknowledge yourself and your circumstances which is indispensable to be able to love somebody else.

4. "Thank you".
   By expressing gratitude with the words 'Thank you', you immediately draw positivity into your life. It is very powerful to thank for future events or for the way you see yourself in the future. By doing that you manifest what is going to be. It means that with your thoughts you can paint your future. This is a very powerful way to draw whatever it is into your life.

You can use this technique in every circumstance of your life, whether it be in a workplace environment, to heal a relationship, to better your financial situation or little things like finding a car park. Whatever negative experience you have or had, look at them as a learning curve. Also be grateful to people you don't get on very well with or people who you can't stand at all, because they all come into our lives to teach us a lesson.

◆ Abundance ◆
Spread your Wings

Look at the four sentences as a kind of mantra that you can repeat throughout the whole day, when you feel your mind drifting off into a negative thought pattern or if something or somebody annoys you, when you are feeling down and unhappy and frustrated, and when you are losing sight of which direction to go.

To practice the four sentences initially, I advise you as always to find a quiet place where you can light a candle, put on soft music or you prefer going for a walk in nature.

I would like to ask you to start with the forgiveness process on yourself. Sit back and look at yourself from outside your body. Notice your persona and look at that person carefully. Maybe the person you look at seems depressed with their shoulders and head hanging. They might send out a sense of heaviness and frustration, unhappiness, etc. Observe the person carefully and then start saying the four sentences with the intention of pure forgiveness.

"I am sorry."
"Please forgive me."
"I love you."
"Thank you."

Keep repeating the words until you become aware of a change in the person you are looking at and when you are happy with the occurred transformation, stop the process and go back into your body and notice how you feel. Repeat the process as often as you think you need to and when you are content within yourself and feel love and acceptance around yourself, then start the process on external problems and people.

Visualise the problem or the person you experience the challenge with and become aware of what you are feeling, seeing and hearing. Tune into your feelings and when they are the most intense, say the four sentences:

"I am sorry."
"Please forgive me."
"I love you."
"Thank you."

While verbalizing the sentences, notice the signs in your body and repeat the sentences until you become aware of a change in your physical body whether it be a sensation of feeling lighter or more at peace or whatever transformation it may be. And again, repeat the process whenever you can and when it comes to mind until you sense being grounded and at peace.

Gratitude

Embrace and be thankful for every second of your existence

If feeling down or sad.

Discover the gift that it holds in every instance.

It might just be as little as a seed.

Fertilise it with only ONE positive thought

Or as little as a smile in the mirror.

Isn't that what we all should be taught?

To draw our happiness nearer and nearer?

Now, make a promise to yourself and no other

To take ownership of your life,

To let the wings do their job,

To be in love with yourself,

To stay true to yourself,

To pull on one string,

To love from within,

To guide and not own your youngsters

And above all,

To enjoy the ride!

Andrea Kimberger-Monairgy

Acknowledgements

1. To my beloved parents, Mama and Papa who brought me into this world and who taught me all the important lessons of life by loving me unconditionally no matter what I did and by being tough in their approach when they were trying to protect me from my own mistakes. Thanks to you, I grew up in an absolute safe environment and was able to develop into a healthy woman with high self-esteem, ready to take on the world. Thank you.

2. My little sister Pips (Birgit), you have been so brave all your life. You got tested so much but always have proven to everybody that you are a real survivor. Thank you for always looking up to me when, in fact, it is up to me to look up to you. You have brought up your two beautiful daughters Sabrina and Corina mostly by yourself from a very young age onwards while working full-time and you have done a marvelous job. Thank you for seeing the fun big sister in me and for acknowledging publicly that you miss me. That makes two of us. I wish we lived closer to each other too because we totally miss out on sharing special occasions with each other. It was so nice to be able to celebrate Nathalie and Beau's wedding together and your input has made this such a special and memorable event for all involved. Thank you.

3. To my beautiful daughter Nathalie who has accompanied me now for twenty-seven years and who has brought out the tougher side in me from time to time as she was growing up. As strong-headed as you can be, as soft, loving and nurturing you are at the same time. You are the kind of daughter a mother can wish for and at the same time, you are a very caring, understanding and protective mother to your darling daughter, my eight-year-old granddaughter

Sofia. Whenever I need support, I know I can count on you and vice versa of course. Thank you for always believing in me.

4. To Beau, my son-in-law, thank you for choosing to live by the side of my daughter. You are a wonderful soul, an enormous caring husband and father and have proven to me many times that you are more than worthy of being with Nathalie.

5. To my second and younger child, my son David who I was able to guide now for almost twenty-one years. You pretty much grew up without family because when you were only eight months old, we left Austria to live here in Australia. I admire you for however having such a beautiful bond with your grandparents, even though you mainly know them from video calling and the visits back home. You have always been the most beautiful, calm and loving nature and as much as you needed me growing up, I know that I can count on you as I am getting older and always find support in you. Thank you.

6. A special mention to a very special friend of mine, who was by my side over the last six years. If it was not for his financial support, this book would have not become a reality. Thank you, Richard for supporting me and having faith in me and my endeavors.

7. I would even like to acknowledge my ex-husband George. From our relationship we were blessed with our amazing children and you made it possible for us to come and live in this abundant, prosperous country Australia which we are proud to call our home now. From the moment we met you spiced my life and we have been through a lot together, all of which makes me to the person I am today. Thank you.

8. With gratitude I think of the many uncles and aunties who always believed in me, who guided me when I needed advice, who supported me in my decisions and who still jump in with a helping hand if I need back up, a very special mention goes to auntie Luise, auntie Henni and uncle Guenter. Thank you for always being there for me.

ACKNOWLEDGEMENTS

9. A very special thanks goes also out to all my cousins and their partners who always make my children and myself welcome on our trips back home. I am the oldest one amongst you and I admire you all (without exception) for what you have achieved in life. Thank you for always having us and for always thinking of us and including us when it comes to family affairs, even though we are thousands and thousands kilometres away on the other half of the globe.

10. To all the people who played an important role in my life, whether it be friends from my parents, my friends back home and my friends here in Australia. A very special mention to my girlfriend Cheryl who has supported me immensely through my toughest times as if I was her own sister. Together with Helen and Kathleen, you made sure that I always kept my head above water and you would be assertive in keeping me moving along. Thank you.

11. Thank you also to my long-term employer ALDI for giving me the opportunity of stepping back into the workforce during the darkest times when I had lost my identity and struggled most. Thanks to my employment with the company I was able to provide for my children and myself and was able to grow as a person. A special thank you to my store managers Richard, Nick, Matthew, and Bec who always had an open ear for me when things got tough and who in the end provided the necessary environment for my development. A huge thank you to my current store manager Paul who makes it possible for me to do my studies and who gives me the time off that I need to grow my coaching praxis. Thank you.

Thank you to all the people who contributed to my journey which led me to find my purpose of serving others and spreading love. I am thinking of Barbara, a psychic who saw my potential for healing people and who put me in touch with Sarah Neil, the lady who trained and attuned me to REIKI, the art of divine channeled healing. In the group she is leading, people pointed me in the direction of healing others by talking to them which first put me on to learn the craft of Conversational Hypnosis, taught by Scott Jansen and finally The Coaching Institute in Melbourne with their founder, the unbelievable inspiring Master Coach Sharon Pearson who shares with us students her profound knowledge and who guides us all to attain the mastery of a fulfilled and happy life with purpose. Thank you, Sharon for all the books you have written and all the programs you put in place to enable the seekers to find their goal. Thank you in the name of all TCI students and thank you for your message "We all have everything we need within ourselves at all times."

12. As part of TCI, I would like to extend my deepest gratitude to the trainers Joe Pane and Matt Lavars who are fully dedicated and committed to making each and every student succeed in their quest to a humble, knowledgeable, respectful, and grateful existence which then results in us finding our life purpose. They are the kind of trainers you can only wish for because besides providing us with immense knowledge, they also know how to hold ourselves accountable to make sure we arrive at our final destination.

13. A huge thank you goes to Shilpa Agarwal and her husband from "Want Solution" because they have been guiding me on my book journey. Without their continuous and supportive advice as my mentors, this book would not exist. Thank you heaps.

14. Thank you to Anthony Robbins and his book "Awaken the Giant Within" which provided me with such a deep insight into the world of how our mind works and how we can use it to create a rewarding and meaningful reality for ourselves. Thank you, you are also my inspiration to becoming a Female Motivational Speaker in the near future.

15. In closing, I would like to extend my gratitude to the Universe which always provides me with all that I need. I am so thankful for my whole family, all my friends here and overseas, work colleagues from both sides of the globe, past and present bosses, teachers, mentors and everybody who I am or was associated with at some point in life. You all have made me in to the person I am today and thanks to you I am able to share my knowledge, commitment and purpose in serving others. What more can one wish for?

Summary

YOUR TREASURE BOX OF MODELS
At this moment in time, please find a summary of all the models that I have been introducing you to as you were reading through my book.

This summary serves you in future when you want to go back to the one or other model in assisting you to work through a new challenge that has arisen for you. I trust that you find it easier that way to pick the perfect solution to your problem with just one look at all the learning examples.

DEDICATIONS

PREAMBLE
Explanation of the book structure and how to read this book

INTRODUCTION – THE ENLIGHTENED WOMEN GENESIS
I now have awareness of
1. Serving myself only
2. Trust and respect for myself and others
3. The belief in myself
4. My purpose
5. Following my happy track at all times
6. Welcoming change
7. Dreaming big
8. How to fly
9. Nurturing my body
10. Feeding my mind and my thoughts' positiveness
11. How to tune into my soul
12. My spiritual awakening

CHAPTER ONE – LEARN YOUR LESSON
THE FOUR STAGE LEARNING JOURNEY
1. Unconsciously Incompetent
2. Unconsciously Competent
3. Consciously Incompetent
4. Consciously Competent

CHAPTER TWO – EARLY SETBACKS TO MAGIC
Who do you have to **BE**?
What do you have to **DO**?
To **HAVE** what you are longing for.

CHAPTER THREE – TAKE OWNERSHIP OF YOUR LIFE
Stay **ABOVE THE LINE** with your thoughts and be responsible for what you are doing and what is happening to you.

Avoid drifting into **BELOW THE LINE** thinking where you are blaming circumstances and others for your reality.

CHAPTER FOUR – LET THE WINGS DO THEIR JOB
TRIAD OF RESULTS:

FOCUS on what you want only and under any circumstances avoid focusing on what you do not want!

Remember to use **LANGUAGE** that works for you:
Use model operators of Possibility: Could, can, like, love to, would
Avoid model operators of Necessity: Have to, got to, must, should, need to

Use your **PHYSIOLOGY** to your advantage, stand up straight, lift your shoulders back and have a smile on your face.

CHAPTER FIVE – THE MEANING OF LOVE – FOR YOUNG AND OLD
ADULT GROWTH MODEL:

To **RELY** in the beginning is okay because when you are learning it is a natural process, you rely on your parents initially, then on your teacher and later in life on your mentors.

SUMMARY

As you grow, you start to REBEL because now you know better, and you start getting

RESULTS and as you keep refining your results, you come to the

REALIZATION that there is even more for you to learn and you go through the whole process again.

The importance is in the movement. Never stagnate because the ultimate standstill is death.

CHAPTER SIX – STAY TRUE TO YOURSELF ALWAYS
VALUES/ENDS - AND MEANS VALUES and RULES:

Remember the difference between Ends and Means Values: Means Values are needed to get you to your Ends Values.
Therefore

MEANS VALUES are: Money, Success, Family, Children, Job, etc.

ENDS VALUES are: Happiness, Joy, Freedom, Independence, Fulfillment, etc.

And then we add Rules to our Values. Be wise in choosing the Rules to your Values because you can make it either easy for yourself or almost impossible to live congruently with your Values by making them depend on too harsh Rules. Be mindful that there are EMPOWERING RULES and DISEMPOWERING RULES.

CHAPTER SEVEN – PULLING ON ONE STRING
BELIEFS:
EMPOWERING BELIEFS versus DIS-EMPOWERING or LIMITING BELIEFS – Which ones do you choose?

BELIEFS as Possibility Filters determining what we allow to enter our mind and what we shut out:
– GENERALIZATION
– DISTORTION
– DELETION

CHAPTER EIGHT – LOVE IS NOT ENOUGH
PAIN VERSUS PLEASURE

Stay in your Comfort Zone and keep feeling your PAIN.
Take one tiny little step over and out of your Comfort Zone and experience PLEASURE.

CHAPTER NINE – WE DON'T OWN THEM/WE ARE HERE TO GUIDE THEM ONLY
3 UNIVERSAL FEARS

- Fear of not being enough
- Fear of not belonging
- Fear of not being loved

For every individual, it is normal to experience fear. The only remedy to cope with fear is to attack it by outstepping your comfort zone and by exercising a daily ritual of gratitude.

CHAPTER TEN – ENJOY THE RIDE
TRUST ME MODEL

Life is an ever-continuing, never-ending journey of growth and learning and this model can be a guide on your way to find out where you are and which way you must go to move forward. The steps to pass through on the way are:
- TRUST
- RELATABILITY
- UNIQUENESS
- SUSTAINABILITY
- TENACITY
- MEANING
- EVOLVE

CHAPTER ELEVEN – FORGIVENESS, YOUR MOST PRECIOUS JEWEL
HO'OPONOPONO

About the author

Andrea Kimberger-Monairgy has overcome a lot of challenges in her life. Her ordeals range from caring for her partner's nine year old daughter and taking in his sixteen year old nephew right in the beginning of their relationship, her children both being born with an anomaly which needed surgical attention, leaving her entire family behind when migrating to Australia and spending more than twenty years in a manipulative relationship which in the end caused her to lose her identity.

She has made it her life purpose to help women all ages who are struggling with similar life crippling issues because she knows that you all deserve the happiest and most fulfilling life at YOUR terms!

In her business RISE ABOVE & BEYOND COACHING & CONSULTING Andrea dedicates her passion and life experience to serving those women in need.

In a four-step process: **Awareness, Approach, Action, Abundance**

She rises Awareness of existing problems or issues,
helps her clients to identify the appropriate Approach and
calls upon Action
until the desired Outcome has been reached by themselves.

Andrea's mantra is according to the title of her book:

"Free Yourself" (Chains Off) and
"Grow Beyond Your Wildest Imagination" (Wings On)

About Rise Above & Beyond Coaching & Consulting

The business name says it all!

Andrea calls upon YOU LADIES to have the courage to change your life circumstances once and for all to the better.

She is a strong believer that you all share in an abundant amount of self-esteem, self-confidence, self-fulfillment, hunger for life, sense of adventure, pride and above all self-love!

She sees it as her mission to encourage and empower you all to guiding you to reach your full potential and to discover your life purpose in the end as the pinnacle of your self-discovery journey.

Ladies – Life is too short to be miserable!!!!!!

According to Andrea, the formula to success is a very simple one:

"Change Your Conditioning – Change Your Circumstances"
"C Y C   C Y C"

If that resonates with you, we must connect!

Flick me an email to andrea@riseaboveandbeyond.com or book your **FREE 60 minute strategy session** at https://bookme.name/riseaboveandbeyond

Direct Contact:
Andrea Kimberger-Monairgy
Australia – 0424 052 427 / International + 61 424 052 427
andrea@riseaboveandbeyond.com

ABOUT RISE ABOVE & BEYOND COACHING & CONSULTING

FIND ME ONLINE

Website:
https://www.riseaboveandbeyond.com

Facebook:
https://www.facebook.com/RiseAboveAndBeyond

RECOMMENDED READING

1. Awaken the Giant Within - Anthony Robbins
2. The Happiness Advantage – Shawn Anchor
3. Ho'oponopono – Dr. Hew Len and Dr. Joe Vitale

www.ingramcontent.com/pod-product-compliance
Lightning Source LLC
Chambersburg PA
CBHW031414290426
44110CB00011B/373